Bertolt Brecht: Plays, Poetry and Prose

Edited by JOHN WILLETT *and* RALPH MANHEIM

The Collected Plays

Volume Seven Part One

Brecht's Plays, Poetry and Prose
annotated and edited in hardback and paperback
by John Willett and Ralph Manheim

The following plays are also available (in paperback only) in unannotated editions:

The Caucasian Chalk Circle; The Days of the Commune; The Life of Galileo; The Measures Taken and other Lehrstücke; The Messingkauf Dialogues; Mr. Puntila and his Man Matti; The Mother; Saint Joan of the Stockyards

Bertolt Brecht Collected Plays

Edited by
John Willett
and Ralph Manheim

The Visions of Simone Machard
Translated by Hugh and Ellen Rank

Schweyk in the Second World War
Translated by William Rowlinson

Methuen · London

First published in this paperback edition in Great Britain in 1985 by Methuen London Ltd, 11 New Fetter Lane, London EC4P 4EE, by arrangement with Suhrkamp Verlag, Frankfurt am Main

Both plays first published in this translation in 1976 by Eyre Methuen as part of Brecht's Collected Plays Volume Seven

Printed in Great Britain by Richard Clay (The Chaucer Press) Ltd, Bungay, Suffolk

ISBN 0 413 58030 X

Contents

Introduction

When Brecht at last arrived in the United States on 21 July 1941 he had just come from the most intensively productive three years of his life as a writer. Starting with the completion of *Fear and Misery of the Third Reich*, they covered the writing of *Galileo*, *Mother Courage*, *Lucullus*, *The Good Person of Szechwan*, *Puntila*, *Arturo Ui*, the *Dialogues between Exiles*, the bulk of *The Messingkauf Dialogues* and the completion and publication of the *Svendborg Poems*. The six American years which were to follow now seem something of a contrast, and they began with several months of uncertainty and near-paralysis as Brecht paused in California wondering where and how to engage his talents. This was due above all to something that had happened on the journey: the death of his aide Margarete Steffin in Moscow from tuberculosis. Both the group of poems which he wrote 'After the death of my collaborator M.S.' (included in *Poems 1913-1956*) and his own private notes and journal entries suggest that this was among the severest blows he ever suffered; in mid-1942 he could write commenting on it:

> for nearly a year i have been feeling deeply depressed as a result of the death of my comrade and collaborator steffin. up to now i have avoided thinking at all deeply about it. i'm not frightened so much of feeling pain as of being ashamed of the fact. but above all i have too few thoughts about it. i know that no pain can offset this loss, that all i can do is close my eyes to it. now and again i have even drunk a tot of whisky when her image rose before me. since i seldom do this even one tot affects me strongly. in my view such methods are just as acceptable as others that are better thought of. they are only external, but this is a problem which i don't see how to resolve internally. death is no good; all is not necessarily for the best. there is no

inscrutable wisdom to be seen in this kind of thing. nothing can make up for it.

As his previous visit in connection with the New York production of *The Mother* had not made him many friends among the American left, virtually the only allies on whom he could now count for help and advice were German anti-Nazi immigrants, mostly of quite recent date. Hanns Eisler the composer had been working at the New School in New York since the beginning of 1938; he was now in the middle of a two-year film music project financed by the Rockefellers. Kurt Weill had arrived in September 1935 and spent some years finding his feet in the New York musical theatre; however at the beginning of 1941 he had successfully established himself on Broadway with the music to *Lady in the Dark*, by Moss Hart and Ira Gershwin, a show which Paramount bought for the record sum of $283,000; from then on he was in a position to choose his own scripts. Piscator had landed on the first day of 1939, and a year later opened his Dramatic Workshop, a theatre school under the wing of the New School; however his attempts to break into the New York professional theatre, starting with a major project for staging *War and Peace*, had come to nothing. Those were the three people to whom Brecht had sent scripts or résumés of the plays written since 1938, and it was thanks to Piscator's approach to the head of the New School that Brecht had been sent the teaching invitation that enabled his family to get its visas for the journey. There were one or two possible translators to whom he sent scripts too, notably Hoffman Hays and Ferdinand Reyher, while in Hollywood he knew German actors and directors such as Fritz Kortner, Peter Lorre, Alexander Granach and the now successful film producer William Dieterle, once a Munich actor. Although Walter Benjamin had killed himself while trying vainly to escape from occupied France in 1940— this being another factor in Brecht's depression —his earliest mentor, the novelist Lion Feuchtwanger, had been more successful and was now established in Pacific Palisades (Los Angeles area) as a literary figure.

Once landed in California, where Granach and Mrs Feuchtwanger came to collect the family at San Pedro docks, Brecht had to decide whether to go on to New York, where there were some signs of interest in the scripts he had sent, or to stay around Los Angeles, where Elisabeth Hauptmann had already approached a number of those friends to promise financial help once he arrived. His choice then lay between an uncertain prospect of getting one or the other of the new plays put on in the theatrical capital in the East and the more rewarding possibility of selling stories and treatments to the motion picture industry in the West. Partly because of the need to earn money, partly because of Feuchtwanger's advice, partly too out of sheer curiosity about what he termed 'the dream factories of Hollywood', he decided to stay put, leaving three plays— *Ui, The Good Person of Szechwan* and *Fear and Misery of the Third Reich*—to find takers in New York, while *Galileo* remained in Reyher's hands in Hollywood. In contrast with Eisler and Weill, who in their different ways felt at home among Americans and enjoyed their respective successes in Hollywood and on Broadway, Brecht was an uncomfortable guest, and the atmosphere of southern Califonria was hardly one to relieve his sense of frustration. This was partly a matter of its utter remoteness from the war—'Tahiti in urban form' he called it soon after arriving—though Pearl Harbor that autumn brought reality closer; partly a deep-seated resentment of its artificiality and underlying commercial ethos. Thus a journal entry of March 1942 (one of many to the same effect):

> extraordinary in these parts how a universally demoralizing cheap prettiness stops one from leading anything like a cultivated, i.e., dignified life.

On top of this came the often degrading experience of working for the films, which bore particularly painfully on him as he became drawn into the making of Fritz Lang's Czech resistance movie *Hangmen Also Die* during the summer of 1942. Taking stock towards the end of April, he listed all the factors hampering him, from his loss of Steffin to his lack of money, and concluded that 'for the first time in ten years i am not doing any proper work'.

Yet even while he was battling over that film (for adequate representation of the Czech people, for his theme song, for a part for Helene Weigel and a scriptwriter's credit for himself:

on all of which points he failed), his outlook in other respects
was beginning to improve. Materially, he and his family no
longer had to live on $120 a month, but were able to move into
a bigger and very much pleasanter house in Santa Monica
(1063 26th Street; it is still there, though the area has been
much built up) on the strength of the $10,000 which Lang got
for him. Once again he was working with Eisler, who had
arrived there in April and for whom he now wrote his
'Hollywood Elegies', condensing much of what he felt about
the civilization around him. He was also in touch with a young
lecturer at UCLA called Eric Bentley, who differed from the
bulk of his friends in being neither central European nor
involved in show-business, and who seems immediately to
have helped him to widen his English reading. From Feuchtwanger he heard that the Zurich Schauspielhaus wished to
stage *The Good Person of Szechwan*, while Thornton Wilder had
seen and been impressed by their production of *Mother
Courage*. Still more changed for him when El Alamein was
followed by Stalingrad (for it should never be forgotten how
closely and continuously Brecht followed the war news). And
during that October he and Feuchtwanger began collaborating on the war play, a modern Saint Joan story, which was to
become *The Visions of Simone Machard*.

*   *   *

First encountered by him in the theatrical form in 1924, when
Max Reinhardt staged Shaw's play in Berlin with Elisabeth
Bergner in the title part, the figure of Joan of Arc fascinated
Brecht right up to the 1950s. There had been the revolutionary
Chicago Salvationist in *Saint Joan of the Stockyards* (unperformed
in Brecht's lifetime but broadcast in 1932), who relates both to
Shen Teh in *The Good Person of Szechwan* and to the heroine of
Happy End; and there was the historic patriot of Anna
Seghers's radio play *The Trial of Joan of Arc at Rouen, 1431* which
was broadcast in 1934 and probably known to Brecht from its
publication in the Moscow German-language *Internationale
Literatur* (later he would adapt it for production in 1952 by the
Berliner Ensemble). There was thus every reason for the saint
to surface again in Brecht's mind in the summer of 1940, as he
worked on *The Good Person of Szechwan* during the collapse of

France and the beginnings, counter to Comintern policy, of the French Resistance. In Finland at that time he noted a plan for a possible play 'to keep one's hand in':

> a young frenchwoman in orléans, working at a filling station while her brother is away, dreams and daydreams of being joan of arc and undergoing her fate. for the germans are advancing on orléans. the voices joan hears are voices of the people—the things the blacksmith and the peasant are saying. she obeys these voices and saves france from the enemy outside, but is conquered by the enemy within. the court that sentences her is packed with pro-english clerics: victory of the fifth column.

Returning to it in America just before Christmas 1941, he sketched out a play in nine scenes under the title *The Voices*, whose social point should be (*a*) that voix dei is really vox populi, and (*b*) that 'owners and criminals stand shoulder to shoulder against anyone who rejects the idea of property'. Exactly at what stage he first discussed this with Feuchtwanger is not clear, but he now laid the plan aside in order to read *The Devil in France*, the book in which the novelist described his own experiences in 1940, when he had been interned outside Aix-en-Provence, then managed to escape across the Pyrenees at the point where Benjamin was turned back. Other readings about the French débâcle followed, though Feuchtwanger, who had spent all the early parts of his exile in that country, remained in essential ways better informed about it than Brecht. Their systematic collaboration began at the end of October, just before the shooting of *Hangmen Also Die*, which Brecht occasionally went to watch in the afternoons. They worked mostly in Feuchtwanger's house, a quiet Spanish-style mansion on the mountains overlooking Santa Monica and the sea, which has now been made over to the University of Southern California. The curfew imposed after Pearl Harbor, together with their status as enemy aliens, prevented their meeting at night.

In one way the work went easily. The two men got on well together, and despite their disagreement as to Simone's age (for which see the notes, pp. 156 and 179) the division of responsibility seems to have given no trouble. Brecht set up the play's structure, which was then filled out in discussion between them—Feuchtwanger evidently doing his best to see that the events were probable and the details authentic—after which the actual writing of the scenes would be done by Brecht and checked over at the next meeting. 'He has a good sense of structure,' wrote Brecht approvingly,

> appreciates linguistic refinements, is also capable of making poetic and dramaturgical suggestions, knows a lot about literature, pays attention to arguments and is pleasant to deal with, a good friend.

at the same time, however, he

> wants to have nothing to do with the technical or social aspects (epic, portrayal, a-effect, characters made up of social rather than biological ingredients, class conflicts built into the story and so on), and tolerates all that merely as my personal style . . .

Perhaps because of the effect of the previous fifteen months of largely pointless work ('that kind of thing can indeed be bad for one's handwriting,' he noted of the role allotted by Hollywood to its authors) Brecht was less able than usual to resist the pressure of convention, for aside from the dream element (itself not particularly daring by local standards) the play is quite Aristotelian in its observation of the unities. Moreover the collaborators almost certainly had Hollywood's demands in mind, both in the play and in the somewhat pot-boiling novel which Feuchwanger subsequently wrote on the same theme (it appeared in 1944 and is briefly summarized on p. 178 ff.). Before Brecht left for New York in February 1943, leaving the ending of the play still not finally settled, an agreement was drawn up between himself, Ruth Berlau (who is neither named as a collaborator nor known to have had any direct role in the work), and the Feuchtwangers, dividing the stage and screen rights equally and giving Feuchtwanger all rights to the proposed novel. Thereafter William Dieterle took an interest, and arranged for a rough translation into English, which had been completed by April. On the strength of this (so Feuchtwanger then wrote to Brecht) the agents Curtis Brown were hoping to persuade either Ashley Dukes or the Muirs to make a good English version. At Columbia Pictures the story editor was favourably impressed. Not so Hanns Eisler, who had watched the development of the play throughout and made occasional suggestions, and was now embarking on the music. He told Brecht in May that he disliked Simone's instinctive patriotism and saw her as the poor victim of a patriotic upbringing. Brecht had failed to show that she was being exploited.

*   *   *

Fate (or the historical dialectic) had it that no sooner was the Saint Joan figure off Brecht's drawing-board than she was replaced by her opposite number in his military thinking: the deeply unpatriotic and subversive Czech anti-hero Švejk. He too had preoccupied Brecht ever since the 1920s, when the German translation of Jaroslav Hasek's great novel first appeared—a full translation, incidentally, such as only became available in English in the 1970s—and his 'tone' too can be identified in a number of Brecht's characters, ranging from Galy Gay in 1926 to Mother Courage and Puntila's man Matti shortly before their author's journey to the United States. The difference here was that Švejk was by no means an obsession special to Brecht but one that was widely shared among mid-European writers of his generation; indeed it formed a bond between them. He was common for instance to all those allies on whom Brecht had at first relied: Eisler, who had set a passage from the novel in his early *Tagebuch des Hanns Eisler*; Weill, who had been involved with Cheryl Crawford of the Group Theatre in stimulating and setting Paul Green's Švejk-based play *Johnny Johnson*; above all, Piscator, who with the help of Brecht and George Grosz had achieved the classic stage realisation of the novel in 1928 and had continually been trying to repeat its success on stage or screen—in Moscow in the early 1930s, in Paris later, and now in 1943 in New York. By then he felt that he had established a moral, if not seigneurial right to produce Hašek's work.

Over the years Brecht and Piscator had intermittently been in touch about various Švejk plans, and no doubt it was the research involved in writing the *Hangmen Also Die* story, with its Prague setting, that rekindled the former's interest and led him to note in July 1942 that

> once again i would like to do *Schweyk*, interspersed with
> scenes from [Karl Kraus's] *The Last Days of Mankind* so
> people can see the ruling forces up top with the private
> soldier down below surviving all their vast plans.

The man who actually got him to work on this project,
however, was not Piscator but his old rival Ernst-Josef
Aufricht, the former Berlin impresario who had first staged
The Threepenny Opera in 1928 and was now in New York after
escaping from Unoccupied France. Partly involved in the
Office of War Information German broadcasts, Aufricht was
also on the lookout for a libretto to interest Kurt Weill, who
must have told him of his search for something suitable. He
helped to put on a mixed programme at Hunter College (in
New York) on 3 April in which Weill and Lotte Lenya
performed some of the Brecht songs, including 'Und was
bekam des Soldaten Weib?' which Weill had recently set; this
finished with a turn by the Czech clowns George Voskovec
and Jan Werich entitled 'Švejk's spirit lives on'. At some point
he reintroduced the two former collaborators, and proposed
that they should make a Švejk musical, quickly raising the
necessary $85,000 from émigrés who remembered their
previous success. Everyone hoped it would be like another
Threepenny Opera.

True as it may be to say, like his biographer Ron Sanders,
that *Lady in the Dark* completed Weill's 'transformation into an
American composer' there was a less prudent part of him
which still seemed to hanker after the texts that only Brecht
could write. Even the great hit in the last of the dream
sequences which that work contained bore the nostalgic title
'The Saga of Jenny', and it looks as if Weill must have been
captivated by the script of *The Good Person of Szechwan* even
before Aufricht brought him together with Brecht once more,
since in the first place he thought of producing that play—i.e.
acting as its impresario, if not actual backer—rather than just
converting it into his next libretto. At the same time, while
discussing musical collaborations with a number of non-
American writers including Georg Kaiser and Bernard
Shaw—this via Gabriel Pascal, who already had the germ of

My Fair Lady in mind—Weill had also embarked on his next major Broadway plan for a production with Cheryl Crawford based on a nineteenth-century story by F. Anstey of *Vice Versa* fame. Written by S.J. Perelman and Ogden Nash and intended in the first place as a vehicle for Marlene Dietrich (who found it too undignified for her), this became the highly successful *One Touch of Venus* whose rehearsals began in the summer of 1943. Aufricht's *Švejk* project thus evidently ranked lower on Weill's scale of priorities than Brecht for one believed, even though the *Good Person* was quickly relegated to a place in the queue behind it. Nevertheless, Brecht thought it urgent, and he spent a week with Weill and Lenya during his visit to New York that spring, writing them not only an outline adaptation of the *Good Person* 'for here' but also the 'Story' of his proposed *Schweyk in the Second World War* (pp. 183-192 below) which he would now go back to California and put into effect.

Having reread Hasek's novel in the train to Los Angeles, he arrived home on 26 May and almost immediately settled down to work on the play. Three scenes were finished by 9 June, the whole script by the end of that month; and, as our notes show, it was very close to the final text. Moreover while it is quite untrue to say as Aufricht dismissively does (in his memoirs) that 'Brecht had copied whole pages of dialogue from the Švejk book', the work flowed very much more easily than *Simone Machard* and seems to have suffered from none of the awkward changes and compromises which mar that play. Brecht himself thought well enough of it to compare it not only with *Mother Courage* but also with

> the schwejk which i wrote for piscator around 27 (a pure montage based on the novel). the present second world war version is a lot sharper and corresponds to the shift from the hapsburgs' well-ensconced tyranny to the invasion by the nazis.

Whether or not this satisfaction was justified—a point which will be discussed later—there were three good reasons why Brecht should have had reservations. First of all, as he knew quite well, Piscator had been talking to the Theatre Guild about the possibility of updating that earlier script, for which he wanted Brecht's assistance; seemingly he had been told

nothing of the Aufricht-Weill plan. Secondly, although
Brecht's new version was in accordance with the outline, and
included a new major character specially devised by him to
engage Lenya's under-used talents, it was nothing remotely
resembling the book and lyrics of a Broadway musical, but
rather a play with music. Thirdly, not only did Weill have
plenty of financially more rewarding things to do, but he had a
citizenship hearing coming up—he was actually sworn in on
27 August—and any political concessions to Brecht's inter-
pretation of Švejk might have counted against him.

Between these three rocks the Good Ship Švejk soon
foundered. Treating his text as much more important than
the Americanised *Good Person*, which he was quite willing to let
Weill have adapted by an American writer, Brecht started by
objecting to the composer's extensive rights in the proposed
contract. 'I'm not a librettist', he told Ruth Berlau on
26 June:

> It has got to be my play, which it is (not just an American
> version, as with the Szechwan play), and it's not only
> America I have to think of. What's more, there are political
> considerations involved in this play; I have to have an equal
> voice.

Not long after, he and Weill met again in Hollywood to
discuss things. Then at the beginning of July he sent the script
to Weill, assuring him that it was not especially important that
(the now differently-spelt) Schweyk himself should talk as he
does in the German version of the novel, where he speaks a
now-defunct kind of Prague German. Paul Selver's translation, he found, had managed to be comic without this, and
without attempting to find Anglo-Saxon equivalents for the
social and political setting. He recommended getting the
American poet Alfred Kreymborg to do a version of the play,
saying that he was known to Ruth Berlau and 'has the right
sort of opinions (liberal)'. It is not clear whether Weill agreed,
though apparently he was already nervous that the script
might prove too un-American for Broadway. Brecht, however,
went ahead and commissioned Kreymborg, paying him out of
a loan from his friend the actor Peter Lorre, who he hoped
might play the name part. The translation was finished by 4

September, all except for the 'Moldau Song', which Brecht himself was still struggling to get right. The unavoidable effect however was to infuriate Piscator, who not only regarded *Schweyk* almost as his own property—and indeed had spent much time in negotiations with the Hašek lawyer, who now gave the rights to Aufricht—but had been expecting Kreymborg to translate the 1928 version for the Theater Guild. On 23 September each of the collaborators got a stiff letter from him, in English, warning them that he had asked his lawyers to protect his rights.

Whether or not Piscator's friendship with Weill was a factor, there was an understanding on Broadway that composers and writers would no longer pursue a project if the rights were disputed. And in any case the finished play never appealed to Weill. Despite assurances that the landlady's part had been written for Lotte Lenya and that he was welcome to get in an American lyric-writer for the songs, he refused to compose a note until the production was definitely fixed, so that by September Brecht had begun discussing alternative plans with Hanns Eisler. Nor did Weill pursue *The Good Person of Szechwan* project further, though Brecht had by then completed the American version and still hoped that they might come to a formal agreement. Yet, though Aufricht too had evidently rather lost heart, Brecht none the less went carefully over Kreymborg's translation when it arrived and sent it back to New York for him and Ruth Berlau to revise. This had been done by the time of Brecht's return to New York in mid-November. Shortly afterwards Weill, now in California with the successful première of *One Touch of Venus* behind him, wrote to Brecht to summarize his objections. He could only collaborate, he said, on three conditions:

1. if the play is written by a top-class American author in the Ben Hecht category and put on by a top-class American producer.
2. if Lenya plays the publican.
3. if the play is written as a 'musical play', with more openings for music than the present version, as I do not under any circumstances wish to write incidental music.

As it stood, he thought that it

> has no prospect of succeeding on the American stage
> without major alterations, unless there is some prominent
> American author (in the Ben Hecht category) who can find
> a way of rendering the humour of your script in American
> terms. Nor do I think the rights position clear enough to
> ensure the backing for a first-class Broadway production.
> But these are entirely private opinions, and I'm only telling
> you them because I don't want you to waste time and
> energy on a project which in my view hasn't much
> chance.

Similarly with *The Good Person of Szechwan*, where any agreement must be conditional on getting hold of an American
writer. Their 'collaboration on the present version of Szechwan' was now at an end.

*   *   *

From Brecht's point of view both *Schweyk* and *Simone Machard*
were now effectively blocked, the former because Broadway
would henceforward fight shy of it, the latter because Metro-
Goldwyn-Mayer bought up the stage rights when they decided
to make the Brecht-Feuchtwanger story into a film. Goldwyn
characteristically had not been able to understand the compli-
cations of the play when he was given it by one Jo Swerling on
Feuchtwanger's behalf, but in February 1944 he bought the
novel rights and Feuchtwanger unquestionably shared his
$50,000 with Brecht. The film, as it turned out, was never
made: initially because Theresa Wright, the designated
Simone, was expecting a baby, and then because the allied
invasion of France that summer destroyed the story's topical
relevance. Similarly with *Schweyk*; for all the interest shown by
Lorre and subsequently by Laughton, who read the English
translation in April the same year, there seems to have been no
further talk of a production. Even those colleges and university
drama departments who were soon to seize on *The Good Person*
and *The Caucasian Chalk Circle* are not known to have staged
either of Brecht's two Second World War plays until the later
1960s, partly no doubt because of the fading topical interest
and partly due to the lack of available translations. Nor did he

himself propose to include them in the English-language edition of his plays which Reynal and Hitchcock were planning to publish in the US around 1946, a plan which was soon to be dropped when another publisher took that firm over. Perhaps he did not by then believe enough in either of them to keep them near the surface of his mind during the intensive work first on *The Caucasian Circle* and later on the adaptation and production of *Galileo* with Laughton. Not that the situation was all that different once he had returned to Europe in the autumn of 1947, for he took no steps to stage either play himself and in both cases the world première took place after his death.

Schweyk in the Second World War, then, was first performed twelve years after the war had ended by the Warsaw Treatr Dramatyczny in a Polish translation by Andrzej Wirth; a number of other East European productions followed. *Simone Machard* had its première that same year at the main Frankfurt municipal theatre in a production by Harry Buckwitz, a courageous and conscientious Brecht director who gave *Schweyk* its West German première at the same theatre two years later. In both cases Eisler had already begun writing the music in California, then given up when it appeared that neither play was about to be produced. Now he completed the songs and wrote in quasi-symphonic, non-Brechtian style for the dream or 'higher' interludes, of which there were four in each play. In both Frankfurt productions Teo Otto designed the sets; likewise with subsequent productions by Buckwitz in other West German theatres. Meantime there was no rush to stage either play at the Berliner Ensemble: in the case of *Schweyk*, once Lorre had rejected the idea Brecht himself had preferred to wait for the right actor to mature or to come along, and in the event Erich Engel directed it at the end of 1962 as his very last (but not very memorable) production; while in the case of *Simone Machard* there has been no production at all. As for Britain, there was a scrupulous *Schweyk* at the Mermaid in 1963 directed by Frank Dunlop, with Bernard Miles in the title part, while *Simone Machard* was performed at the old Unity Theatre two years earlier, and subsequently by the Glasgow Citizens' Theatre in late February 1967.

Today we can see that the obstacles to the effective performance of these two plays lie not in any uncertainty about rights or actors but in their own weaknesses. Perhaps *Simone Machard* is not as bad as it seemed at the time to Brecht's friends Aufricht and Hans Borchardt, who advised him in New York to put his script straight into the wastepaper basket; but the form of the play is still conventional, the figure of the heroine imprecise and the French characterisation generally artificial. In practical terms too it demands an extravagantly large cast, and the dream interludes are not easy to stage. These last two points apply equally to *Schweyk*, although this play is at least centred on a classically memorable character and contains many stories, incidents and Švejkian turns of phrase to make an inexperienced audience laugh. That said, however, the whole notion of pitting Hašek's beautifully ambiguous figure (balanced as he is between simple idiocy and subtle insubordination) against Himmler and the SS is a deep misconception which distorts both recent history and Hašek's novel. As Jan Kott pointed out in his review of the Warsaw première, the Austrian monarchy was funny despite all, whereas Hitler and the Nazis were not: 'in the Second World War the Švejks always lost out'. If this error of judgement and of political sensitivity on the playwright's part must have been disturbing to those who had been up against the Nazis themselves, it can be positively damaging to those who have not. For the trouble in more sheltered countries like our own is that it has become so common for the entertainment media to adopt a jokey attitude towards humanity's recent enemies that Švejk easily slots into the pattern of hilarious wartime sitcom, as seen for instance in the TV series *Hogan's Heroes* with its laughable Nazis. Far as this was from Brecht's ultimate intentions it sticks out as one of the most obvious opportunities presented by the part and the play, and the more brilliantly it is seized (as it was in Richard Eyre's production for the National Theatre in 1982 with Bill Paterson as Schweyk) the remoter the audience will be from the horrible truth. On such occasions laughter is in no way constructive, as true satire must be. It is escapist, a witless insult to war's victims.

Both plays were conceived for a market with which Brecht was not familiar, America at war; and they suffer from this in two ways. Because they are structurally unoriginal, using Hollywood-style jumps into fantasy rather than epic narration, they lack the new momentum that distinguished the Piscator *Schweyk* of 1928. At the same time they aim to bring their basic themes up to date—the Saint Joan story in one case, Hašek's anti-militarist satire in the other—relocating their two protagonists in the context of the war against the Nazis. And in so doing they destroy their credibility. Each of course contains many incidental beauties and shrewd observations, but there is not so much lasting relevance in them as in those plays which Brecht situated more remotely and wrote with greater detachment. There could be a lesson here for those directors who seek to add topical references to Brecht's work in the hope of making it mean more to a modern audience. Such changes can falsify the relationships on which a play's long-term message depends.

The Visions of Simone Machard

This play was written in collaboration with LION FEUCHT-
WANGER

Translators: HUGH AND ELLEN RANK

Characters

Philippe Chavez, mayor of Saint-Martin (in the dream scenes,
King Charles VII) · Henri Soupeau, *Patron* of the hostelry (the
Connétable) · Marie Soupeau, his mother (Isabeau the Queen
Mother) · Capitaine Honoré Fétain, a rich vineyard proprietor
(the Duke of Burgundy) · The Colonel (Bishop of Beauvais) ·
A German *Hauptmann* (an English general)
Simone Machard (in the dream scenes, Maid of Orléans) · The
drivers Maurice and Robert, Georges, Père Gustave, all
employees of the hostelry · Madame Machard, Monsieur
Machard, Simone's parents · A sergeant · Refugees · Minor
personages (in the dream scenes, soldiers and crowd) · The
angel

The scene is the courtyard of the Hostellerie 'Au Relais'. A
low garage forms the background. Stage right, the back
entrance to the hostelry; left, the store room with attics for the
drivers. Between the garage and the store room there is a
widish gateway giving on the street. The garage is capacious
since the hostelry is at the same time a transport business. The
action takes place in June 1940 in the little town of Saint-
Martin in central France on one of the main roads from Paris
to the South.

THE BOOK

The soldier Georges, his right arm bandaged, sits smoking next to old Père Gustave who is repairing a tyre. The brothers Maurice and Robert, the two chauffeurs from the hostelry, are staring at the sky. Noise of aeroplanes. It is the 14th of June, evening.

ROBERT: Those must be ours.

MAURICE: They aren't ours.

ROBERT *calling to Georges:* Georges, are those ours or German?

GEORGES *moving his bandanged arm cautiously:* The top part of my arm has gone numb too now.

PÈRE GUSTAVE: Don't move it; that's bad for it.

Enter Simone Machard, a girl in her teens. Her apron is too long, her shoes too large. She is dragging a very heavy basket full of washing.

ROBERT: Heavy?

Simone nods and drags the basket to the foot of the petrol pump. The men go on smoking and watch her.

GEORGES *to Père Gustave:* D'you think it could be the bandage? It's gone stiffer since yesterday.

PÈRE GUSTAVE: Simone, get Monsieur Georges some cider from the shed.

SIMONE *putting down her basket:* Suppose the *Patron* sees us.

PÈRE GUSTAVE: Do as you're told.

Exit Simone.

ROBERT *to Georges:* Why don't you answer? Fancy wearing a uniform and not even looking up when there are planes about. If all our soldiers are like you, you bet we'll lose the war.

GEORGES: What do you say to that, Robert? The top part of my arm has gone dead too now. Père Gustave thinks it's just the bandage.

ROBERT: I asked you what planes those are overhead.

GEORGES *without looking up:* German. Ours stay on the ground.

Simone has returned with a bottle of cider and pours some of it out for Georges.

SIMONE: Do you think we'll lose the war, Monsieur Georges?

GEORGES: Whether we lose or win I'll be needing two arms.

Monsieur Henri Soupeau, the Patron, enters from the street. Simone quickly hides the cider. The Patron stops in the gateway; he looks to see who is in the courtyard and beckons towards the street. A gentleman in a large dustcoat enters. The Patron shows him across the yard, taking considerable trouble to screen him from the gaze of the others; the two disappear into the hostelry.

PÈRE GUSTAVE: Did you see that chap in the dustcoat? He's an officer. A colonel. Another of those who have run away from the front. They don't want to be seen. Yet they eat enough for three.

Simone has gone to her basket and sat down by the petrol pump. She starts to read a book which was lying on top of the basket.

GEORGES: I'm annoyed with Robert. According to him they're bound to lose the war if all our soldiers are like me. But thanks to me they've won other things, that's for sure. Thanks to my boots for example some gentleman in Tours has made a nice profit and thanks to my helmet a gentleman in Bordeaux has done the same. My tunic brought in a château for someone on the Côte d'Azur, and my gaiters brought in seven racehorses. That way France did pretty well out of me long before the war arrived.

PÈRE GUSTAVE: But the war is being lost. By those dust-coats.

GEORGES: Yes, we've two hundred hangars with a thousand fighter planes, all paid for and fully manned, test-flown; but now that France is in peril they stay on the ground. The Maginot Line cost a hundred million and is made of steel and concrete with seven storeys below ground in open countryside. And when the battle began the Colonel got into his car and drove to the rear, followed by two lorry-loads of wine and provisions. Two million men were waiting for orders, ready to die, but the War Minister's mistress had fallen out with the Prime Minister's mistress, so no order came. Well, our strongpoints are immovably fixed in the ground, their strongpoints are mobile and roll right over us. Nothing can stop their tanks as long as they have fuel, and the fuel they just come and get from our pumps. Tomorrow morning they'll be here in front of your petrol station helping themselves freely. Thanks for the cider.

ROBERT: Don't talk about tanks—*with a nod towards Simone*— when she's around. Her brother is at the front.

GEORGES: She's buried in her book.

PÈRE GUSTAVE: A game of cards?

ROBERT: I've got a headache. We've been driving the Captain's wine barrels all day through streams of refugees. A mass migration.

PÈRE GUSTAVE: The Captain's wine is the most important refugee of the lot. Don't you understand that?

GEORGES: Everybody knows the man's a fascist. He must have heard from his mates on the general staff that something has gone wrong again at the front.

ROBERT: Maurice is furious. He says he's fed up with driving those bloody wine barrels through all those women and children. I'm going to have a kip. *Exit.*

PÈRE GUSTAVE: You can't run a war with streams of refugees like that. The tanks can get through any ordinary bog, but a bog of people gets them stuck. The civil population seems to be a great liability in this war. It ought to have been shifted to another planet before they started, it's nothing but a nuisance. You have to abolish people or abolish war, you can't have them both.

GEORGES *has sat down next to Simone and puts his hand into the laundry basket:* But you've taken the washing off the line dripping wet!

SIMONE *reading on:* The refugees keep pinching the table-cloths.

GEORGES: Probably for nappies or to wrap their feet in.

SIMONE: But Madame keeps check of them.

GEORGES *pointing to her book:* Still reading about Joan of Arc? *Simone nods.* Who gave you that book?

SIMONE: The *Patron.* But I can't get down to reading. I'm still on page 72 where Joan finishes off the English and crowns the King in Rheims. *She reads on.*

GEORGES: What are you reading that old-fashioned stuff for?

SIMONE: I want to know what happens next.—Is it true that France is the most beautiful country in the whole world, Monsieur Georges?

GEORGES: Is that what it says in the book? *Simone nods.* I don't know the whole world. But they say the most beautiful country is the country you live in.

SIMONE: What's the Gironde like, for instance?

GEORGES: I believe that's another place where they grow wine. France is the great wine-drinker, so they say.

SIMONE: Are there a lot of barges on the Seine?

GEORGES: About a thousand.

SIMONE: And Saint-Denis, where you used to work: what's it like there?

GEORGES: Nothing to shout about.

SIMONE: Apart from that it's the most beautiful country.

GEORGES: It's a good country for bread, wine and fish. There's nothing wrong with the cafés with their orange awnings or the huge meat and fruit markets, especially in the morning. The bistros where you sit over a glass of Framboise aren't so bad either. The fairs and ship launchings with brass bands, we could keep them too. Who could have anything against the poplars people play boules under? Do you have to go down to the village hall again today with those food packets?

SIMONE: I wish the sappers would arrive before I have to go.

GEORGES: What sappers?

SIMONE: They're expecting some sappers in the kitchen. Their field kitchen got lost among those streams of refugees, and they're from 132 Regiment.

GEORGES: That's your brother's lot, isn't it?

SIMONE: Yes. They're moving up to the front.—This book

says the Angel told the Maid to kill all France's enemies, it was God's will.

GEORGES: You'll have nightmares again if you read that gory stuff. What do you think I took the newspapers away from you for?

SIMONE: Do their tanks really go right through the crowds, Monsieur Georges?

GEORGES: Yes. And you've read enough.

He tries to take her book away. The Patron appears at the door of the inn.

PATRON: Georges, you're not to let anyone into the breakfast room. *To Simone:* And you're reading again during working hours, Simone. That's not what I gave you the book for.

SIMONE *has busily begun to count the tablecloths:* I only glanced at it while I was counting the linen. Sorry, Monsieur Henri.

PÈRE GUSTAVE: If I were you I wouldn't have given her that book, Monsieur Henri. It makes her quite confused.

PATRON: Nonsense. In times like these it won't hurt her to learn something about French history. Our young people don't know what France means any longer. *Speaks over his shoulder into the house:* Jean, the hors-d'œuvres into the breakfast room. *Turns to those in the yard:* You read and see what sort of a spirit there was then! God knows we could do with another Maid.

PÈRE GUSTAVE *with a hypocritical air:* Where could we find one?

PATRON: Where could we find one? Anywhere! It could be anyone. You. Georges. *Pointing to Simone:* It could be her. A child could tell you what's needed, it's obvious. Even she could tell our country.

PÈRE GUSTAVE: A bit small for a Joan of Arc perhaps.

PATRON: A bit small, a bit young, a bit tall, a bit old! There's always a good excuse when the spirit is lacking. *Over his shoulder, back into the house:* Did you take some of the Portuguese sardines, Jean?

PÈRE GUSTAVE: Well, what about it? Do you feel like a change? Only I'm afraid angels don't appear these days.

PATRON: That's enough, Père Gustave. I would be obliged if you suppressed your cynicism in the presence of this child. Let her read her book without your dirty comments. *Going in:* But it needn't be in working hours, Simone. *Exit.*

PÈRE GUSTAVE *grinning:* How about that, Georges? Now even the scullery maid is to be re-educated to become the Maid of Orléans, just in her spare time of course. They are stuffing the children with patriotism. They themselves are hiding in their dustcoats; or hoarding their petrol in some brickworks we know of instead of handing it over to the army.

SIMONE: The *Patron* wouldn't do anything wrong.

PÈRE GUSTAVE: No, he's the great benefactor. He pays you twenty francs a week so that your people should 'have at least that much'.

SIMONE: He's keeping me on so my brother doesn't lose his job here.

PÈRE GUSTAVE: In that way he gets a petrol pump attendant, a waitress and a scullery maid, all rolled into one.

SIMONE: That's because there's a war on.

PÈRE GUSTAVE: And that's not at all bad for him, is it?

PATRON *appears in the doorway of the hostelry:* Père Gustave, half a bottle of Chablis '23 for the gentleman who's having trout. *Returns into the hostelry.*

PÈRE GUSTAVE: The gentleman in the dustcoat, alias the Colonel, desires a bottle of Chablis before France falls. *Exit into the store room. During the following scene he brings the bottle of Chablis across the yard into the hostelry.*

A FEMALE VOICE *from the first floor of the hostelry:* Simone, where are the tablecloths? *Simone takes up the basket and is about to enter the hostelry. Enter from the street a sergeant and two sappers with a dixie.*

SERGEANT: We're supposed to pick up our food here. The Mayor's office say they've rung up.

SIMONE *keen, radiantly:* I'm sure it'll be ready. Just go into the kitchen. *To the sergeant, while the two sappers go in:* My brother

André's with 132 Regiment too, Monsieur. Do you happen
to know why there has been no more mail from him?

SERGEANT: Everything is upside down at the front. We
haven't been in touch with our people at the front for the
last two days either.

SIMONE: Have we lost the war, Monsieur?

SERGEANT: Oh no, Mademoiselle. It's just a question of
isolated thrusts by enemy tank formations. They think the
monsters will soon run out of petrol. Then they'll just break
down along the roads, you know.

SIMONE: I've heard they won't get as far as the Loire.

SERGEANT: No, no. Don't you worry. It's a long way from
the Seine to the Loire. The only bad thing is those streams
of refugees. You can hardly move because of them. And
we have to repair the bombed bridges, otherwise our reserves can't get through.

The two sappers return with their dixie, the sergeant looks into it.

SERGEANT: Is that all? It's a disgrace. Look at this dixie,
Mademoiselle. Not even half full. This is the third restaurant they've sent us to. Nothing at all in the first two, and
now this.

SIMONE *looks into the dixie, shocked:* That must be a mistake.
We've got enough. Lentils, bacon too. I'll go and see the
Patron myself straight away. You'll get a full dixie. Wait a
moment. *She runs in.*

GEORGES *offering cigarettes:* Her brother can't be more than
seventeen. He was the only volunteer in Saint-Martin.
She's very fond of him.

SERGEANT: The devil take it, I don't call this a war. They're
treating the army like an enemy in its own country. And the
Prime Minister saying on the radio 'The Army is the
People'.

PÈRE GUSTAVE *who has come out again:* 'The Army is the
People.' And the people are the enemy.

SERGEANT *hostile:* How do you mean?

GEORGES *looking into the cauldron:* How can you stand for
that? Fetch the Mayor.

SERGEANT: We know Mayors. They do nothing.

SIMONE *returns slowly, without looking at the Sergeant:* The *Patron* says that's all the hostelry can spare; there are so many refugees.

PÈRE GUSTAVE: And we can't spare anything for them because the army gets it all.

SIMONE *desperately:* The *Patron* is furious because the Mayor's office is making such demands.

SERGEANT *tired:* Always the same story.

PATRON *in the doorway, handing a folded bill to Simone:* Give the gentleman who had trout his bill. Tell him I'm charging the strawberries at what they cost me, it was your parents that sold them to the hostelry. *He pushes her in.* What's the matter? Are the gentlemen not satisfied? Perhaps you'll be good enough to put yourselves in the shoes of the civil population. They have already been bled white, and new demands are being put on them all the time. God knows nobody feels for France as I do, but—*with a great gesture of helplessness*—I can only keep this place up by making the greatest sacrifices. Look at the help I've got. *Points to Père Gustave and Georges.* An old man and a cripple. And this youngster of a girl. I give them work because otherwise they would starve. But I can't feed the French army as well.

SERGEANT: And I can't ask my men to march into the night under fire for you on an empty stomach. Mend the bridges yourselves. I'll wait for my field kitchen. Even if it means waiting seven years. *Exit with sappers.*

PATRON: What can I do? You can't please everybody. *Trying to ingratiate himself:* Well, boys, you should be glad you don't own a hostelry. It's like having to defend it against wolves, eh? After all the trouble we took to get it two stars in the guide book. *With annoyance, as Père Gustave and Georges show little sympathy for his troubles:* Don't stand around like cabbages! *Calling back into the house:* Monsieur, the yard is clear now.

COLONEL, *the gentleman in the dustcoat, comes out of the hostelry; to the Patron who sees him across the yard as far as the street:*

Your prices are impudent, Monsieur. 160 francs for a lunch!

GEORGES *has meanwhile gone into the hostelry and pulls out Simone, who holds her hands to her face:* They left quite a while ago. You don't have to hide in the passage because of them. It's not your fault, Simone.

SIMONE *drying her tears:* It's just that they're from the 132nd too, you know. Their people at the front are waiting for help, and the sappers have to repair the bridges first, Monsieur Georges.

PATRON *returning from the street:* Foie gras, trout, saddle of lamb, asparagus, Chablis, coffee, a Martell '84. In these days! And when the bill comes they pull a face that long. But they have to be served at the double because they can't wait to get away from the battle. An officer! A colonel! Poor France. *Observing Simone, and with a bad conscience:* And you, don't you interfere in kitchen matters. *Exit into the hostelry.*

GEORGES *to Père Gustave, pointing to Simone:* She's ashamed because of the sappers.

SIMONE: What are they going to think of the hostelry, Monsieur Georges?

GEORGES *to Simone:* It's not you who ought to be ashamed. The hostelry cheats like hell, the *Patron* would take the pennies off a dead man's eyes. You aren't the hostelry, Simone. When they praise the wine you have no reason to smile and when the roof falls in you have no reason to cry. It wasn't you chose the linen. It wasn't you held back the food. Get me?

SIMONE *unconvinced:* Yes, Monsieur Georges.

GEORGES: André's fully aware you are keeping his job here warm for him. That's enough. Now you go off to the village hall and see young François. But don't let his mother scare you again with her talk of Stukas, or you'll dream half the night that you're in the middle of the fighting. *He pushes her into the hostelry. To Père Gustave:* Too much imagination.

PÈRE GUSTAVE *mending his tyre:* She doesn't like going down

to the hall. They abuse her because the food packets are too
expensive.

GEORGES *with a sigh:* She will even stick up for the *Patron*, if
I know. She's loyal, our Simone.

PATRON *comes out of the hostelry and calls in the direction of the
store room, clapping his hands:* Maurice! Robert!

ROBERT'S VOICE *from the shed, sleepily:* Yes?

PATRON: Captain Fétain rang up. He wants you to go on to
Bordeaux with the rest of his wine barrels.

ROBERT'S VOICE: Tonight? But that's impossible, Monsieur Henri. We've been two days on the road.

PATRON: I know, I know. What can I do? The Captain thinks
we're taking too long about it. What do you expect, with
those blocked roads? I really don't want to do you out of
your sleep, but . . . *Gesture of helplessness.*

ROBERT'S VOICE: But the roads are blocked by night too,
and on top of that you can't use your headlights.

PATRON: That's war for you. But we can't antagonize our
best customers. Maman insists on it. So get ready. *To Père
Gustave:* Oh, do finish your tyre.

*Monsieur Chavez, the Mayor, has entered from the street, a brief-
case under his arm. He is very agitated.*

PÈRE GUSTAVE *drawing the Patron's attention to him:* The
Mayor.

MAYOR: Henri, I've got to speak to you once more about
your lorries. I must insist that you put them at my disposal
for the refugees.

PATRON: But I've told you that I'm bound by contract to
move Captain Fétain's wine. I can't say no to him. Maman
and the Captain have been friends from their young days.

MAYOR: Captain Fétain's wine! Henri, you know how I hate
to interfere in your business affairs, but under present conditions I can no longer make allowances for your relations
with that fascist Fétain.

*Simone has come out of the hostelry with a tray full of big packets
suspended from her neck and carrying two baskets filled with more
packets.*

PATRON *menacingly:* Philippe, better not call Captain Fétain a fascist.

MAYOR *bitterly:* 'Better not.' That's all you've got to say, you and your Captain, when the Germans are up to the Loire. France is going to the dogs.

PATRON: Where? Where are the Germans?

MAYOR *emphatically:* Up to the Loire. And our Ninth Army, which was standing by to relieve the situation, has found Route 20 blocked with refugees. Your lorries are requisitioned like all the other lorries in Saint-Martin, and will be ready tomorrow morning to evacuate the refugees in the hall. That's official. *He takes a small red notice from his brief-case and is about to stick it to the garage door.*

SIMONE *quietly, horrified, to Georges:* The tanks are coming, Monsieur Georges!

GEORGES *putting his arm round her shoulder:* Yes, Simone.

SIMONE: They're up to the Loire; they'll be coming into Tours.

GEORGES: Yes, Simone.

SIMONE: And they will be coming here, won't they?

PATRON: Now I understand why the Captain was in such a hurry.

Shaken: The Germans up to the Loire, that's terrible. *Crosses over to the Mayor, who is still busy fixing his notice.* Philippe, leave that. Let's go in. We must talk in private.

MAYOR *angrily:* No, Henri, we are not going to talk in private any more. Your people are to know that your lorries have been requisitioned, and your petrol too. I've winked an eye for too long.

PATRON: Have you gone mad? Requisitioning my lorries at this juncture! And I have no petrol except that little bit here.

MAYOR: Plus some black market stuff you haven't registered.

PATRON: What? You dare suspect me of hoarding petrol illegally? Père Gustave, have we any black market petrol? *Père Gustave pretends not to have heard, and is about to roll his tyre into the garage.*

PATRON *shouting:* Maurice! Robert! Come down at once! Père Gustave! *Père Gustave stops.* Out with it! Have we any black market petrol or not?

PÈRE GUSTAVE: I don't know anything about it. *To Simone, who is staring at him:* You get on with your work and stop eavesdropping.

PATRON: Maurice! Robert! Where are you?

MAYOR: If you have no extra petrol how are you going to move Captain Fétain's wine?

PATRON: A catch question, eh, Mayor? Well, I'll tell you: I'm going to move the Captain's wine with the Captain's petrol. Georges, have you heard of my having any black market petrol?

GEORGES *looking at his arm:* I've only been back from the front four days.

PATRON: All right, that lets you out, but here are Maurice and Robert. *Maurice and Robert have come.* Maurice and Robert! Here's Monsieur Chavez accusing the hostelry of hiding petrol. I ask you in Monsieur Chavez's presence: is that true? *The brothers hesitate.*

MAYOR: Maurice and Robert, you know me. I'm no policeman. I don't like interfering in other people's business. But France needs petrol now, and I am asking you formally to state that there is petrol here. You are honest chaps.

PATRON: Well?

MAURICE *gloomily:* We don't know about any petrol.

MAYOR: So that's your answer. *To Simone:* You've got a brother at the front. But I suppose you won't tell me there is petrol here either.

Simone stands motionless, then she begins to cry.

PATRON: Ah, you want to call this young girl as a witness against me? You have no right, Mayor, to undermine this child's respect for her *Patron. To Simone:* You can go.

MAYOR *tired:* Are you sending her to the hall again with those exorbitant packets of yours? You gave the sappers a half-empty dixie. Everybody's exploiting the refugees down to their last sou, that's why they can't move on.

PATRON: I am an innkeeper, not a charitable institution.

MAYOR: All right. Only a miracle can save France now. She's rotten to the core. *Exit. Silence.*

PATRON: Beat it, Simone. Allez hopp!

Simone walks slowly and uncertainly to the gateway of the yard, repeatedly looking round. The book which she has hidden on her tray drops to the ground. She shyly picks it up and walks out of the yard with her packets and baskets.

First Dream of Simone Machard

Night of 14–15 June

Music. Out of the darkness the angel emerges. He stands on the garage roof, his face golden and expressionless. In his hand he has a small drum, and he calls out 'Joan!' three times in a loud voice. Then the stage gets lighter, and Simone is standing in the empty courtyard looking up at the angel, with the linen basket on her arm.

THE ANGEL

Joan, thou daughter of France, something must be done
Or mighty France will bleed to death before two weeks
    have run.
That's why God Almighty has begun looking around for
    aid
And now His eyes have fallen on His little Maid.
I bring you a drum, which God's sent specially
For you to shake the people awake from their everyday
    lethargy.
To beat it so that it echoes you must lay it on the ground
As if you would make the very soil of France resound
Till rich and poor, old and young, all waking from their
    trance
Take pity on their mother, la France.

If she needs shipping, summon every bargeman on the
Seine.

Make the peasants of Gironde feed her fighting men.

When she wants tanks you must wake the metal workers in
the town of Saint-Denis.

Let the carpenters of Lyon saw away the bridges to hamper
the enemy.

Speak to them. Tell them that the mother by whom they've
been protected

And whom in return they have insulted and rejected—

Tell them that France, the mighty worker and drinker of
wine

Needs them to rescue her. Let your drumming be their sign!

SIMONE *looking round to see if anyone else is there:* Do I have to,
Monsieur? Aren't I too small for a Saint Joan?

THE ANGEL: No.

SIMONE: Then I'll do it.

THE ANGEL: It will be hard. Leftit cribble clump.

SIMONE *timidly:* Are you my brother André?

The angel is silent.

SIMONE: Are you all right?

*The angel disappears. But Georges comes sauntering out of the
darkened garage, bringing Simone his bayonet and his steel helmet.*

GEORGES: A sword and a helmet, that's what you'll need.
It's not the sort of thing for you, but the *Patron* has nobody
else to help him apart from a cripple and a young girl. Forget about your work. Listen, the tanks are going ahead like
bulldozers, flattening everything. No wonder your brother
is now an angel.

SIMONE *taking the helmet and bayonet:* Shall I clean them for
you, Monsieur Georges?

GEORGES: No, as you're the Maid of Orleans you'll need
them.

SIMONE *putting on the helmet:* How right you are. I must go
straightaway and see the King at Orleans. It's a good
twenty miles, the tanks do about 45 m.p.h., and my shoes
are full of holes, I shan't have a new pair till Easter. *Turns as*

if to go. At least wave me good-bye, Monsieur Georges, or else I'll be too scared to go; battles are old-fashioned, bloody stuff.

Georges makes an effort at waving with his bandaged arm, then disappears. Simone sets out on her way to Orleans, marching around in a small circle.

SIMONE *sings loudly:*

As I went to Saint-Nazaire

I forgot my trousers.

All at once I heard a cry:

Where've you put your trousers?

I replied: at Saint-Nazaire

Skies are blue as ever

And the wheat's as tall as I

And the sky blue as ever.

The drivers Maurice and Robert suddenly appear jogging along after her, bearing medieval weapons but in their overalls.

SIMONE: What are you doing here? Why are you following me?

ROBERT: We're following you because we are your body-guard. But would you mind not singing that song, it's indecent. After all, we are engaged to you, Joan, so you'd better behave yourself.

SIMONE: Am I engaged to Maurice too?

MAURICE: Yes, secretly.

Père Gustave comes towards them dressed in very simple medieval armour. He looks away and tries to pass them.

SIMONE: Père Gustave!

PÈRE GUSTAVE: Count me out. Fancy putting me in the heavy artillery at my age. What a nerve! Live off tips and die for France!

SIMONE *quietly:* But your mother, France, is in *danger*.

PÈRE GUSTAVE: My mother was Madame Poirot the washer-woman. She was going to get pneumonia. But what could I do? I couldn't afford all the dozens of medicines she needed.

SIMONE *shouting:* Then I command you in the name of God

and the Angel to turn back and command the heavy artillery against the enemy. *More softly:* I'll clean it for you.

PÈRE GUSTAVE: All right, that's different. Here you are, take my pike. *He adds his pike to her load and joins them in their march.*

MAURICE: How much longer, Simone? We're doing this for the bloated capitalists. Workers of unfurled, ignite! *Simone replies likewise in dream language and is incomprehensible to the audience. She speaks with great conviction.*

MAURICE *who understands her:* That's quite true. Good, let's march on.

ROBERT: You're stumbling, Simone. This load is too heavy for you.

SIMONE *suddenly quite exhausted:* Sorry. But I didn't have a proper breakfast. *Stops and wipes her brow.* I'll be all right in a minute. Robert, can you remember what I'm to tell the King?

ROBERT *says something in the incomprehensible dream language, then:* That's all.

SIMONE: Many thanks. Of course. Look, over there—the towers of Orleans.

The Colonel arrives wearing armour under his dustcoat. He slinks across the yard and out.

PÈRE GUSTAVE: That's a fine start. The brasshats are clearing off; they're on the run.

SIMONE: Why are the streets so empty, Père Gustave?

PÈRE GUSTAVE: Probably all at supper.

SIMONE: And why hasn't anyone rung the alarm bells now the enemy's on the doorstep, Père Gustave?

PÈRE GUSTAVE: They were probably sent to Bordeaux on Captain Fétain's orders.

The Patron stands at the entrance of the hostelry wearing a helmet with red plumes and an improvised shining breastplate.

PATRON: Joan, take these exorbitant packets down to the hall straightaway.

SIMONE: But Monsieur Henri, our beloved mother France is in danger. The Germans are up to the Loire and I must talk to the King.

PATRON: Are you mad? I'm doing all I can. Don't forget I'm the *Patron*. Your duty is to me.

A man dressed in crimson emerges from the garage.

SIMONE *proudly:* Look, Monsieur Henri, here comes King Charles VII!

The man in crimson is actually the Mayor, who is wearing the royal robe over his suit.

MAYOR: Hullo, Joan.

SIMONE *astonished:* Are you really the King?

MAYOR: Yes, that's official, I'm confiscating the lorries. We must talk in private, Joan.

The drivers, Père Gustave and the Patron disappear into the darkness. Simone and the Mayor sit down at the foot of the petrol pump.

MAYOR: Joan, all is lost. The General's gone off without leaving an address. I've written to the Connétable to ask for artillery, but the letter with my royal seal was returned unopened. My Master of Horse says he's been wounded in the arm, but if that's so nobody has seen it. Everything is rotten to the core. *Weeping:* I suppose you have come to tax me with being weak. Well, so I am. But what about you, Joan? First of all, tell me where the black market petrol is kept.

SIMONE: In the brickworks of course.

MAYOR: I knew it, I winked an eye; but you're robbing the refugees down to their last sou with your exorbitant packets.

SIMONE: It's because I have to keep an angel's job warm for him, King Charles.

MAYOR: And it's to keep their job that the drivers transport Captain Fétain's wine rather than refugees?

SIMONE: Also because the *Patron* says they're on essential work, so they aren't called up.

MAYOR: O dear, the innkeepers and the nobility, that's who I have to thank for my grey hairs. The nobility is against the King. It says that in your book. But you have the people behind you, particularly Maurice. Shall we make a pact, Joan, you and me?

SIMONE: Why not, King Charles? *Hesitantly:* But you'd have

to interfere quite drastically in business matters if the dixies are to be kept full.

MAYOR: I'll see what I can do. However, I must tread carefully, or they'll cut off my royal income. I'm the man who always winks an eye, and so of course nobody does what I say. I'm expected to do all the dirty work. Take the sappers, for instance. Instead of simply taking their food from the hostelry by force, they come to me and say 'Mend the bridges yourselves. *We'*ll wait for our field kitchen.' It's not surprising then if the Duke of Burgundy goes over to the English.

PATRON *in the doorway:* I understand your Majesty is not satisfied. Perhaps you'll be good enough to put yourself in the shoes of your civil population. They've already been bled white. Nobody feels for France more than I do, but . . . *Gesture of helplessness. Exit.*

MAYOR *resignedly:* How can we beat the English like that?

SIMONE: The time has come for me to sound my drum. *She sits down on the ground and beats her invisible drum. Every beat resounds as if it were emanating from the bowels of the earth.* Arise, bargemen of the Seine! Follow me, metal workers of Saint-Denis! You carpenters of Lyons, wake up! The enemy is coming!

MAYOR: What are you looking at, Joan?

SIMONE: They are coming! Don't flinch! At their head is the drummer with a voice like a wolf and a drum stretched with a Jew's skin; clinging to his shoulders, a vulture with the look of the banker Fauche from Lyons. Just behind him comes Field-Marshal Fireraiser. He is on foot, a fat clown wearing seven uniforms not one of which makes him look human. Swinging above the heads of these two fiends is a canopy of newspapers, making him easily recognizable. Behind them ride the hangmen and the generals. Each one has a swastika branded on his low forehead, and following them as far as the eye can see come the tanks and guns and railway trains, also lorries with altars on and torture chambers, for everything is on wheels and highly mobile. Ahead go the battle waggons and behind come the loot waggons. The people are mown down, but the harvest is brought in. So wherever they arrive cities collapse, and wherever they have been a barren waste remains. But now there will be an end of them, for here stands King Charles and the Maid of God, that's me.

All the French characters who have already appeared in the play and others yet to appear group together on the stage, carrying medieval weapons and wearing improvised armour.

SIMONE *radiantly:* You see, King Charles, they're all here.

MAYOR: Not all, Joan. I don't see my mother Isabeau, for example, and the Connétable went away in anger.

SIMONE: Don't be afraid. I must crown you King so that we have unity among the French. I remembered to bring your crown. Here it is. *She takes a crown from her linen basket.*

MAYOR: Who am I going to play cards with if the Connétable doesn't come back?

SIMONE: Okkal grisht burlap.

Simone places the crown on the Mayor's head. In the background appear the sappers beating their dixie with a ladle. Great ringing of bells.

MAYOR: Why are the bells ringing?

SIMONE: Those are the bells of Rheims cathedral.

MAYOR: Aren't they the sappers I sent to the hostelry to collect their food?

SIMONE: They didn't get any. That's why their dixies are empty. Those empty dixies are your coronation bells, King Charles.

MAYOR: Clether dunk freer! Clicketick!

ALL: Long live the King and the Maid who crowned him!

MAYOR *to Simone:* Thank you very much, Joan, you have saved France.

The stage darkens. The voice of a radio announcer mingles with a cacophony of music.

THE HANDSHAKE

Early morning. The drivers Maurice and Robert, Père Gustave and the soldier Georges are sitting at breakfast. Sound of the wireless from the hostelry.

RADIO: We are repeating a bulletin released by the Ministry of War at 3.30 a.m. Owing to the unexpected crossing of the Loire by German tank formations, fresh streams of refugees have been pouring along strategically vital roads in central France tonight. The population is urgently requested to stay put so that the roads can be kept open for our relief forces.

MAURICE: It's time to scram.

GEORGES: The head waiter and the others have gone; they spent the whole night packing the china, then they pissed off. The *Patron* threatened them with the police, but it made no difference.

ROBERT *to Georges:* Why didn't you wake *us* right away?
Georges does not reply.

MAURICE: The *Patron* didn't let you, eh? *He laughs.*

ROBERT: Aren't you clearing off too, Georges?

GEORGES: No. I'll get rid of my uniform and stay put. At least I get something to eat here. I've given up hoping my arm will ever be all right.
The Patron comes out of the hostelry. He is smartly dressed and appears to be very busy. Simone shuffles after him, carrying his suitcases.

PATRON *clapping his hands:* Maurice, Robert, Gustave, come along, come along. Get this china on to the lorries. Everything in the store room goes too. Pack the hams in salt. But first load up my best wines. You can drink your coffee later, there's a war on. We're going to Bordeaux.
They ignore him and continue with their breakfast. Maurice laughs.

PATRON: What's the matter? Didn't you hear me? The things must be packed and put on the lorries.

MAURICE *off-handedly:* The lorries have been requisitioned.

PATRON: Requisitioned? Rubbish. *With a great gesture:* That was yesterday. The German tanks are rumbling towards Saint-Martin. That changes everything. What applied yesterday doesn't apply today.

PÈRE GUSTAVE *murmurs:* Too true.

PATRON: Take that cup away from your mouth when I'm talking to you.

Simone has put down the suitcases and during this exchange has quietly returned to the hostelry.

MAURICE: Another coffee, Robert.

ROBERT: Right you are; you never know where the next one's coming from.

PATRON *trying to suppress his anger:* Have some sense. Help your *Patron* to pack up. I'll see you right. *As none of them looks up:* Père Gustave, go and get started on the china. Get a move on.

PÈRE GUSTAVE *gets up hesitantly:* I'm still eating my breakfast. Don't look at me like that. That won't work any more. *Angrily:* You can stuff your bloody china, today. *Sits down.*

PATRON: Have you gone crazy too? At your age? *He looks from one to the other, then notices the motorbike; bitterly:* Oh, I see, so you're waiting for the Germans? Your *Patron's* finished? So that's the love and respect you owe to your provider. *To the drivers:* Three times I declared you indispensable; otherwise you'd be at the front now. And that's the thanks I get. That's what comes of thinking we're all one little family. *Over his shoulder:* Simone, a cognac! I feel quite weak. *As there is no answer:* Simone, where the devil are you?—Now she's gone too.

Simone comes out of the hostelry wearing a jacket over her dress. She tries to leave without being seen by the Patron.

PATRON: Simone!

Simone continues on her way.

PATRON: Have you gone mad? Answer me.

Simone starts running; exit. Patron shrugs his shoulders and taps his forehead.

GEORGES: What's the matter with Simone?

PATRON *turning to the drivers again:* So you're refusing to work for me, eh?

MAURICE: Not a bit. When we've done eating, we're off.

PATRON: And the china?

MAURICE: We'll take it. If you load it up.

PATRON: Me?

MAURICE: Yes, you. It's yours, isn't it?

ROBERT: But we can't guarantee we'll get to Bordeaux, Maurice.

MAURICE: Who can guarantee anything today?

PATRON: That's monstrous! Do you know what will happen to you if you disobey orders here in the face of the enemy? I'll have you put up against a wall and shot.

Simone's parents enter from the street.

PATRON: What do *you* want?

MADAME MACHARD: We've come because of our Simone. They say the Germans will be here soon and you are leaving. Simone is only a young girl, and Monsieur Machard is worried about the twenty francs a week.

PATRON: She's run away, God knows where.

GEORGES: Hasn't she come home, Madame Machard?

MADAME MACHARD: No, Monsieur Georges.

GEORGES: That's strange.

The Mayor comes in with two policemen. Simone is hiding behind them.

PATRON: Just in time, Philippe. *With a great gesture:* Philippe, I've got a mutiny on my hands. Do something.

MAYOR: Henri, Mademoiselle Machard tells me you are planning to make off with the lorries. I shall prevent this unlawful act with all the means at my disposal. That includes the police. *Points to the policemen.*

PATRON: Simone, have you had the impertinence ... ? Gentlemen, in the kindness of my heart I gave this creature a job for her parents' sake.

MADAME MACHARD *shaking Simone:* What have you done now?

Simone remains silent.

MAURICE: I sent her.

PATRON: I see. And you obeyed *Maurice*?

MADAME MACHARD: Simone, how could you?

SIMONE: I wanted to help Monsieur le Maire, Maman. They need our lorries.

PATRON: *Our* lorries!

SIMONE *becoming confused:* The roads are blocked for André, you see. *Unable to go on:* Please, Monsieur le Maire, you explain.

MAYOR: Henri, do try to be a bit less selfish. The child was right to call me. In times like these whatever we have belongs to France. My sons are at the front, so is her brother. Not even our sons belong to us any more.

PATRON *outraged:* So there's no more law and order? So private property has ceased to exist, has it? Why don't you hand over my hostelry to the Machards? Perhaps these gentlemen, my drivers, would like to empty my safe? This is what I call anarchy! May I remind you, Monsieur Chavez, that my mother went to school with the Préfet's wife? And there's still a telephone.

MAYOR *more weakly:* Henri. I'm only doing my duty.

PATRON: Philippe, be logical. You talk about what belongs to France. Don't my provisions, my valuable china, my silver belong to France? Would you like to see them fall into the hands of the Germans? Not a coffee cup, not a tin of sardines, not a single sausage must fall into enemy hands. They must find a desert, I hope you remember that. You as mayor should come to me and say: Henri, it's your duty to get all your possessions to safety. To which I'd have to reply: Philippe, to do that I need my lorries.

Agitated voices of a crowd from the street. The bell of the hotel is being rung and a door being hammered.

PATRON: What's that? Georges, go and see what's happening *Georges goes into the hostelry.* And as for my employees, who have so far forgotten themselves as to abandon my possessions, you should say—*to the drivers:* Gentlemen, I am appealing to you as Frenchmen to pack the china.

GEORGES *coming back:* A crowd of people from the village hall, Monsieur Henri. They've heard a rumour that the lorries are to be taken away. They're very upset and want to speak to the Mayor.

PATRON *growing pale:* There you are, Philippe. I have Simone to thank for that. Quick, Georges, close the gate. *Georges goes to do so.* Quick, quick, hurry up!—That's the effect of that vicious propaganda against my packets. The mob. *To the policemen:* Do something! Quickly! You must phone for reinforcements, Philippe, you owe me that. They'll do things to me, Philippe. Help me! Please, Philippe.

MAYOR *to his policemen:* Guard the gate. *To the Patron:* Nonsense, nothing's going to happen to you. You heard what he said, they just want to speak to me. *Responding to a fresh hammering at the yard gate:* Let a deputation in. No more than three.

The policemen open the gate slightly and negotiate with the crowd. Then they admit three people, two men and a mother with a child in arms.

MAYOR: What is it?

ONE OF THE REFUGEES *excitedly:* Monsieur le Maire, we've got to have those lorries.

PATRON: Didn't you hear that the roads must be kept free?

WOMAN: For you? While we have to wait here for the German bombers, is that it?

MAYOR *to the refugees:* Madame, Messieurs, don't panic. The lorries are all right. The hostelry just wants to save some valuable property from the threat of enemy action.

WOMAN *indignantly:* There you are! They want to evacuate crates, not people.

A noise of aeroplanes can be heard.

VOICES *from outside:* Stukas!

PATRON: They're diving.

The noise becomes louder and louder. The planes have dived. Every-body throws himself to the ground.

PATRON *when the planes have gone:* One could get killed that way. I must be off.

VOICES *from outside:* Hand over the lorries! Are we supposed to stay here and die?

PATRON: And the stuff hasn't been loaded! Philippe!

SIMONE *angrily:* This isn't the time to think of your pro-visions!

PATRON *astounded:* What's come over you, Simone?

SIMONE: At least we could give those people the food.

THE REFUGEE: Ah, it's food? Is it food they're trying to get away?

MAURICE: That's it.

WOMAN: And there wasn't even a drop of soup for us this morning.

MAURICE: It's the French he's trying to keep his food from, not the Germans.

WOMAN *runs back to the gate:* Open up, you! *As the policemen hold her back she shouts over the wall:* It's the hostelry's food stocks that's supposed to be going on the lorries!

PATRON: Philippe! Don't let her broadcast it.

VOICES *from outside:* They're sneaking out the food!—Break open the gate!—Aren't there any men here?—The idea is evacuate the food and leave us to the mercy of the German tanks!

The refugees break the gate in. The Mayor goes towards them.

MAYOR: Messieurs, Mesdames, no violence please! Every thing will be all right.

While the Mayor is negotiating at the gate a violent slanging-match breaks out in the courtyard. Two main groups form: on one side the Patron, the first Refugee and the Woman, together with Simone's parents, on the other Simone, the drivers, the other refugee and Père Gustave. Georges takes no part in the proceedings but carries on with his breakfast. Old Madame Soupeau has meanwhile come out of the hostelry unnoticed. She is very old and dressed entirely in black.

WOMAN: At least eighty people with no chance of transport.

PATRON: They'll take their bundles with them, Madame; why should I leave everything behind, they're my lorries, aren't they?

MAYOR: How much room do you need, Monsieur Soupeau?

PATRON: For at least sixty crates. Then the other lorry could take some thirty refugees.

WOMAN: So you'd leave fifty of us behind, would you?

MAYOR: What about managing with half a lorry, so that at least the children and the sick can go?

WOMAN: Do you mean to split up families? You wicked man!

PATRON: Another eight or ten could sit on the crates. *To Madame Machard:* I have your daughter to thank for this.

WOMAN: That child has more of a heart than all the rest of you put together.

MADAME MACHARD: Please excuse our Simone, Monsieur Henri. She got those ideas from her brother, it's dreadful.

SIMONE: You know the roads and can take a roundabout way so as to leave Route 20 clear for the troops.

ROBERT: Catch us driving his stuff through Noah's Flood!

SIMONE: But you'll take the sick and the children, won't you?

ROBERT: The refugees are a different matter.

PÈRE GUSTAVE: You keep out of it, Simone, that's my advice to you.

SIMONE: But our beautiful France is in grave danger, Père Gustave.

PÈRE GUSTAVE: She got that out of that damned book of hers. 'Is not our beautiful France in danger?'

ROBERT: Madame Soupeau's come down. She is beckoning you.
Simone goes to Madame Soupeau.

WOMAN *to the crowd at the gate:* Why don't we take the lorries, and the food too?

MADAME SOUPEAU: Simone, take this key and give these people as much food as they want. Père Gustave, Georges, you give them a hand.

MAYOR *loudly:* Bravo, Madame Soupeau!

PATRON: Maman, how can you? What are you doing down here anyway? You could catch your death in this draught. And our cellars have got 70,000 francs' worth of food and fine wines in them.

MADAME SOUPEAU *to the Mayor:* It is all at the disposal of the Saint-Martin council. *To the Patron, coldly:* Would you rather it was looted?

SIMONE *to the woman with the baby:* You'll get the food.

MADAME SOUPEAU: Simone! My son has followed your suggestion and just put the hostelry's entire stock of food at the disposal of the council. That leaves only the china and the silver, which will take up very little room. Is anybody going to load it for us?

WOMAN: And what about making room for us in the lorries?

MADAME SOUPEAU: Madame, we shall take as many of you as possible, and the hostelry will be honoured to feed those who stay behind.

THE FIRST REFUGEE *calling back towards the gate:* Would old Monsieur and Madame Creveux and the Meunier family stay behind if they're certain to get fed here?

CALL FROM THE BACKGROUND: It's possible, Jean.

WOMAN: Just a minute, if we're going to be fed here I want to stay behind too.

MADAME SOUPEAU: You will be welcome.

MAYOR *in the gateway:* Messieurs, Mesdames, help yourselves. The hostelry's stocks are at your disposal.

Some of the refugees move hesitantly towards the store room.

MADAME SOUPEAU: And bring us a few bottles of cognac, Simone, the 1884 Martell.

SIMONE: Very well, Madame. *She beckons to the refugees and goes into the store room with them, Père Gustave and Georges.*

PATRON: This will be the death of me, Maman.

ONE OF THE REFUGEES *drags out a crate of provisions with Georges's help and cheerfully mimics a street seller:* Fruit, ham, chocolate! Provisions for your journey! All free today!

PATRON *looking indignantly at the tins which Georges and the refugee are carrying across the yard towards the street:* Oh, my delicacies! That's foie gras!

MADAME SOUPEAU *softly:* Shut up. *To the refugee, politely:* I hope you enjoy it, Monsieur. *The other refugee, with Père Gustave's help, is dragging baskets full of food across the yard.*

PATRON *lamenting:* My 1915 Pommard! And there goes my caviar! And there . . .

MAYOR: There are times when one must make sacrifices, Henri. *Sceptically:* It's a matter of showing good will.

MAURICE *imitating the Patron's anguish:* 'My Pommard!' *He bursts out laughing and slaps Simone on the shoulder.* I'll load your china, Simone, for a sight like that!

PATRON *offended:* What's so funny ? *Pointing to the disappearing baskets:* That's looting.

ROBERT *good-naturedly, carrying a basket:* Don't take it to heart, Monsieur Henri. Your china will get loaded all right.

MADAME SOUPEAU: Agreed. *She takes some tins and bottles of wine to Simone's parents.* Help yourselves. You too. Glasses for your parents, Simone.
Simone gives them glasses, then she takes a stool, puts it up against the wall and hands food from one of the baskets to the refugees on the other side.

MADAME SOUPEAU: Maurice, Robert, Père Gustave, get yourselves glasses too. *With a glance at the policemen:* I see the force is already equipped. *To the woman with the baby:* Take a sip with us, Madame. *To everybody:* Mesdames, Messieurs, let us raise our glasses to the future of our beautiful France.

PATRON *standing alone and apart from the rest:* What about me ? *Fills a glass and joins the others.*

MAYOR *to Madame Soupeau:* Madame, in the name of the Saint-Martin council I thank the hostelry for its generous contribution. *Raising his glass:* To France. To our future.

GEORGES: Where's Simone?

Simone is still busy passing food over the wall to the refugees.

MAYOR: Simone!

Simone approaches, flushed and hesitating.

MADAME SOUPEAU: Yes, you must have a glass too, Simone. We all owe you a debt of gratitude.

They all drink.

PATRON *to the drivers:* Friends again? Do you really think I was so set against taking the refugees? Maurice, Robert, I am an obstinate man but I can appreciate noble motives when I see them. I don't mind admitting my faults. You should do the same. Let's forget our little personal squabbles and firmly close our ranks against the common enemy. We'll shake hands on it.

The Patron starts with Robert, who shakes his hand with a sheepish smile; then Georges gives him his left hand. Then the Patron embraces the woman with the baby. Père Gustave, still angry, grumbles as he shakes hands. Then the Patron turns to the driver Maurice. Maurice makes no attempt to give him his hand.

PATRON: Oho! Are we all Frenchmen or aren't we?

SIMONE *reproachfully:* Maurice!

MAURICE *shakes hands with reluctance. Ironically:* Long live our new Saint Joan, unifier of the French!

Monsieur Machard boxes Simone's ears.

MADAME MACHARD: That's for your obstinacy in knowing better than the Patron.

PATRON *to Machard:* No, Monsieur, you shouldn't have done that. *He embraces Simone and comforts her.* Simone's my pet, Madame. I've a soft spot for her. *To the drivers:* But let's start loading up, boys. I'm sure Monsieur Machard will lend a hand too.

MAYOR *to his policemen:* How about your helping Monsieur Soupeau?

PATRON *with a deep bow to the woman with the baby:* Madame! *They disperse, as does the crowd outside. Only the Patron, the Mayor, Madame Soupeau, Simone, the two drivers and Georges remain on the stage.*

PATRON: Boys, I wouldn't have missed this for anything. Devil take the caviar and the Pommard. All I want is unity!

MAURICE: And what about the brickworks?

PATRON *whose sore spot this is:* What about it? Well, what? All right, if any of the lorries are low on petrol send them to the brickworks. They can fill up there. Does that make you happy?

ROBERT: In Abbeville the German tanks filled up from the pumps on the road. No wonder they get ahead so fast.

GEORGES: Our 132nd Regiment was overrun by tanks before you could say How's your father? Two battalions wiped out in no time.

SIMONE *terrified:* Not the Seventh?

GEORGES: No, not the Seventh.

MAYOR: All stocks of petrol must be destroyed, Henri.

PATRON: Aren't you jumping the gun? One can't destroy everything just like that. We may still drive the enemy back. Eh, Simone? Tell Monsieur Chavez that France isn't lost yet, not by a long chalk. *To Madame Soupeau:* Well, it's au revoir, Maman. It worries me to leave you behind. *He kisses her.* But Simone will look after you. Au revoir, Simone. I'm not ashamed to thank you. You are a good Frenchwoman. *Kisses her.* As long as you're here nothing will fall into German hands, I'm sure. The hostelry must be left bare, we're agreed on that, aren't we? I'm sure you will do everything just as I would wish it. Au revoir, Philippe, old chap. *Embraces him, picks up his own luggage. Simone wants to help him. He waves her aside:* Leave it. Talk to my mother about what should be done with our food stocks.
Exit to the street.

SIMONE *running after the two drivers:* Maurice, Robert! *She kisses them on the cheeks. Maurice and Robert finally leave.*

VOICE OF THE RADIO ANNOUNCER: Attention please! German tank formations have been sighted at Tours. *This announcement is repeated intermittently up to the end of the scene.*

MAYOR *pale, beyond himself:* They could be here tonight.

MADAME SOUPEAU: Don't be such an old woman, Philippe.

SIMONE: Madame, Père Gustave and Georges and I will just run over to the brickworks. We'll destroy the petrol stocks.

MADAME SOUPEAU: You heard what the *Patron* ordered. He asked us to do nothing in a hurry. You must leave some of the decisions to us, my dear.

SIMONE: But Madame, Maurice says the Germans move so quickly.

MADAME SOUPEAU: That's enough, Simone. *Turns to leave.* There's a nasty draught here. *To the Mayor:* Thank you, Philippe, for everything you've done for the hostelry today. *In the doorway:* By the way, Simone, now they've all gone away I'll probably be closing the hostelry down. Give me back the key of the food store. *Simone, deeply hurt, gives her the key.* I think it would be best for you to go home now to your parents. I've been well satisfied with your services.

SIMONE *who cannot understand:* But can't I help when the council comes for the food?

Madame Soupeau, without a further word, disappears into the hostelry.

SIMONE *after a pause, haltingly:* Have I been dismissed, Monsieur le Maire?

MAYOR: I'm afraid so. But don't be offended. You heard her, she's been well satisfied with your services. Coming from her, that means a lot, Simone.

SIMONE *flatly:* Yes, Monsieur le Maire.

Exit Mayor dejectedly. Simone's glance follows him.

Second Dream of Simone Machard

Night of 15–16 June

A confusion of festive music. A waiting group looms out of the darkness: the Mayor in royal robes, the Patron and the Colonel both in armour, carrying field marshals' batons; the Colonel is wearing his dustcoat over his armour.

COLONEL: Our Joan has taken Orléans and Rheims after first clearing the whole length of Route 20 for our troops' advance. We must bestow great honours on her, clearly.

MAYOR: That is my business as King, Monsieur. The dignitaries and great families of France now gathering here will bow deeply before her.

In the background the names and titles of dignitaries and great French families are called out continually till the end of the scene, as though they were assembling.

MAYOR: By the way, didn't I hear she had been dismissed? *Discreetly:* On the express wish of the Queen Mother, the proud Queen Isabeau, I understand.

PATRON: I know nothing about that, I wasn't there. That would be quite unacceptable. Simone is my pet. Of course she'll stay.

The Mayor says something incomprehensible in the dream language, apparently something evasive.

COLONEL: Here she comes.

Simone marches in, wearing a helmet and sword, preceded by her bodyguard consisting of Maurice, Robert and Georges, all dressed in armour. From the darkness Simone's parents have emerged together with the employees of the hostelry, 'the People'. The bodyguard uses its long pikes to thrust them back.

ROBERT: Make way for the Maid!

MADAME MACHARD *craning her neck:* There she is. That helmet quite suits her.

MAYOR *advancing:* Dear Joan, what can we do for you? Wish yourself something.

SIMONE *with a bow:* First of all, King Charles, my beloved home town must continue to be fed from the hostelry's food stores. As you know, I have been sent to help the poor and needy. Taxes are to be remitted.

MAYOR: That goes without saying. What more?

SIMONE: Next, Paris must be taken. The second campaign must commence without delay.

PATRON *astonished:* A second campaign?

COLONEL: What will old Madame Soupeau, the proud Queen Isabeau, have to say to that?

SIMONE: I need an army with which I can decisively defeat the enemy, and I need it this year, King Charles.

MAYOR *smiling:* Dear Joan, we are well satisfied with your services. Coming from us, that means a lot. So be content. You must leave some of the decisions to us. I am now closing the hostelry down, so you can go home. But before that you will of course be raised to the nobility. Lend me your sword (I have mislaid mine) so I may declare you Dame of France.

SIMONE *hands him the sword and kneels:* Here's the key. *The confused music now includes an organ and choir, and suggests festive church ceremonies in the distance. The Mayor solemnly touches Simone's shoulder with the sword.*

BODYGUARD AND PEOPLE: Long live the Maid! Long live the Dame of France!

SIMONE *as the Mayor is about to leave:* One moment, King Charles. You're forgetting to give back my sword. *Urgently:* The English are not defeated yet, and the Burgundians are raising a new army, even more terrifying than their first. The most difficult tasks still lie ahead.

MAYOR: I am greatly obliged to you for your offer. And thank you for everything else, Joan. *Hands over Simone's sword to the Patron.* Take it safely to Bordeaux, Henri. We for our part must talk in private now with old Madame Soupeau, the proud Queen Isabeau. Good-bye, Joan, it was a great pleasure meeting you. *Exit with Patron and Colonel.*

SIMONE *very frightened:* But listen to me, the enemy is coming!

The music dies down to a murmur, the light dims, the crowd disappears in the darkness.

SIMONE *remains still, then:* André! Help me! Descend, archangel! Speak to me! The English are gathering their army, and Burgundy has gone over, and our men are running away.

THE ANGEL *appearing on the garage roof, reproachfully:* Joan, tell me, where has your sword gone?

SIMONE *confused, apologetically:* They dubbed me Dame with it, then they didn't give it back. *Quietly, ashamed:* I've been dismissed.

THE ANGEL: That explains it. *After a silence:* Maid, hear me: don't let them pack you off. Hold out. France demands it. Better not return yet to your parents; they'd worry themselves to a skeleton over your dismissal. Moreover you promised to keep your brother's job in the garage warm for him, because one day he will be returning. Joan, remain here! How could you abandon your divine mission when you know the invader might arrive from one moment to the next?

SIMONE: Should we go on fighting even after the enemy has won?

THE ANGEL: Do you feel the night wind blowing?

SIMONE: Yes.

THE ANGEL: Is there not a tree in the yard?

SIMONE: Yes, the poplar.

THE ANGEL: Do its leaves rustle when the wind blows?

SIMONE: Yes, distinctly.

THE ANGEL: Then you must not quit the fight even if defeated.

SIMONE: But how can I fight if I have no sword?

THE ANGEL:

After the conqueror occupies your town
He must feel he's isolated, on his own.
No one of you must ever permit him to come in:
He can't count as a guest, so treat him like vermin.
No place for him shall be laid, no meal prepared

Every stick of furniture must have disappeared.
Whatever can't be burned has to be hidden
Pour all your milk away, bury each crust of bread as bidden
Till he's screaming: Help me! Till he's known as: Devilry.
Till he's eating: ashes. Till he's living in: débris.
He must be given no mercy, no kind of aid
And your town must be a memory, from the map let it fade.
Let each prospect be blank, every track bare and savage
And provide no vestige of shelter, only dust and sewage.
Go forth now and ravage!
The stage darkens. Above the music the Angel's voice can repeatedly be heard, softly and persistently calling 'Go forth and ravage!' as the rumble of heavy tanks becomes evident.

3

THE FIRE

(a)

Old Madame Soupeau, dressed entirely in black, together with, behind her, Thérèse the chambermaid and Père Gustave in his best suit, are standing at the gate to the yard waiting for the German captain. Georges, now dressed as a civilian, is leaning against the garage in which Simone is hiding from Madame Soupeau and listening to him. Rumbling of passing tanks outside.

SIMONE: She's white as a sheet and scared.

GEORGES: She imagines they're going to take her hostage and then shoot her. She was in a state last night and Thérèse heard her shouting out: 'The butchers will kill us all.' And yet out of sheer greed she stayed, and now she's waiting for the German captain to come.—I can't understand why you don't want her to see you. Is something the matter?

SIMONE *lying:* No, no. But if she sees me she'll send me away. For fear the Germans might do something to me.

GEORGES *distrustfully:* Is that the only reason you don't want her to see you?

SIMONE *changing the subject:* Do you suppose the Germans have caught up with Maurice and Robert?

GEORGES: Maybe.—Tell me, why did you move out of your room in the main building?

SIMONE *lying:* Oh, there's room now in the drivers' quarters. Do you suppose André will be back soon?

GEORGES: I doubt it.—She hasn't dismissed you, has she, Simone?

SIMONE *lying:* No.

GEORGES: Here come the Germans.

From the street comes the German captain, accompanied by Captain Fétain. At the gate Madame Soupeau and the two officers exchange civilities. Their words cannot be distinguished.

GEORGES: That captain and crypto-fascist is taking a real pride in introducing our hereditary enemy to Madame. All very civil to one another. They're sniffing and each seems to find the other's smell all right. Our hereditary enemy is a proper gent, educated too, which is obviously a great relief to Madame. *Whispers:* They're coming this way.

Simone steps back. Madame Soupeau leads the two gentlemen across the yard into the hostelry, with Thérèse the chambermaid following.

PÈRE GUSTAVE *goes over to Georges and Simone after Madame has whispered something to him:* Madame no longer wishes to see that mob from the hall here. It might upset the German gentlemen. As it turns out, the *Patron* might just as well have stayed.

GEORGES: Their first announcement on the radio was 'Those who respect law and order have nothing to fear'.

PÈRE GUSTAVE: That one actually says 'please' when he wants something. 'Please show my batman my rooms.'

SIMONE: All the same, he is the enemy.

Exit Père Gustave into the store room.

GEORGES: Has your cousin had any more dreams?

SIMONE: Yes, last night.

GEORGES: About the Maid again?

SIMONE *nodding:* She's been raised to the nobility.

GEORGES: That must have been a great time for her.

SIMONE: Taxes have been remitted in her home town, just like it says in the book.

GEORGES *quite sharply:* But the hostelry's stores haven't been handed over to the council as promised.

SIMONE *embarrassed:* My cousin didn't say anything about that.

GEORGES: Aha.

SIMONE: Monsieur Georges, if a certain person appears as an angel, as sometimes happens in my cousin's dreams—does it mean the person's dead?

GEORGES: Not necessarily. It only means the dreamer is sometimes afraid he might be dead.—What else has your cousin got to do?

SIMONE: Oh, a whole lot.

GEORGES: Did something unpleasant happen in that dream?

SIMONE: Why?

GEORGES: Because you've so little to say about it.

SIMONE *slowly:* Nothing unpleasant happened.

GEORGES: I only ask because it strikes me a certain somebody might take these dreams seriously, Simone, and forget that we're living in broad daylight and not in a dream.

SIMONE *bursting out:* Then I shan't tell you any more about my cousin's dreams, Monsieur Georges.

The woman with the baby and another refugee come into the court-yard.

SIMONE: They are coming for the food. Break the news to them as gently as you can, Monsieur Georges. *She hides and watches the scene.*

GEORGES *stepping forward:* Madame.

WOMAN: The tanks have arrived.

MAN: There are three of them parked outside the Mairie.

WOMAN: Enormous ones. At least twenty feet long, they are.

MAN *pointing to the German sentry:* Careful.

MADAME SOUPEAU *coming out of the hostelry:* Georges, Père Gustave! Take the Herr Hauptmann his hors-d'œuvres in the breakfast room.—What do you people want?

WOMAN: We've come about the provisions, Madame. Twenty-one people have stayed behind in the hall.

MADAME SOUPEAU: Georges, I've told you to keep beggars away from the hostelry.

MAN: What do you mean: beggars?

MADAME SOUPEAU: Why don't you tell your people that from now on they must deal with the German Kommandant, not with me. The good old days are finished.

WOMAN: Is that what we're supposed to go back and tell the people in the hall, after we have advised them all to stay so you could get your china off?

MADAME SOUPEAU: I would advise you not to inform on me, Madame.

WOMAN: Don't try to hide behind the Germans.

MADAME SOUPEAU *over her shoulder:* Honoré!

WOMAN: The baby and I could have been with my sister in Bordeaux by now. You promised to see we had enough food, Madame.

MADAME SOUPEAU: Because you blackmailed me into it, Madame.

CAPITAINE *appearing behind her:* After a good deal of looting. But now, my friends, law and order will be restored. *Pointing at the German sentries:* Would you like me to have you escorted out under guard? Don't get excited, Marie, remember you have a weak heart.

WOMAN: You're a lot of swine.

MAN *holding her back and leading her away:* Times will change, Madame.

MADAME SOUPEAU: It's starting to stink of sewage here. All the scum of the northern cities flooding into our peaceful villages. We're getting the habitués of the cheapest wine bars. Sooner or later there'll be a bloody reckoning.—Père Gustave, breakfast for four!

CAPITAINE *to Georges:* Here, you! The Mayor will be coming here. Tell him I want a word with him before he sees the Herr Hauptmann. *He leads Madame Soupeau back into the hostelry. When they have both disappeared, Simone runs after the refugees.*

GEORGES: Père Gustave! The hors-d'œuvres for the Herr Hauptmann!

PÈRE GUSTAVE *from the store*: I get it. Only the best for the Herr Hauptmann.

Simone returns breathless.

GEORGES: What did you tell them?

SIMONE: That they can tell the people in the hall that they'll get their food. I'm going to do it tonight.

GEORGES: Of course, you've still got the key.

SIMONE: It was promised them.

GEORGES: Better be careful. That's stealing.

SIMONE: The *Patron* said: 'As long as you're here, Simone, nothing will fall into German hands, I'm sure!'

GEORGES: That's not the way the old lady's talking.

SIMONE: Perhaps they're forcing her.

The Mayor appears at the gate.

SIMONE *flying towards him*: Monsieur le Maire, what are we to do?

MAYOR: How's this, Simone? I've got good news for you: I've put forward your father for a job with the council. You have deserved that, Simone. Then it won't matter so much that you have lost your job.

SIMONE *whispering*: Monsieur le Maire, is it true there are three tanks on the square outside the Mairie? *Even more quietly*: That petrol is still there, you know.

MAYOR *absently*: Yes, that's bad. *Suddenly*: What are you still in the hostelry for, Simone, anyway?

SIMONE: Surely something must be done about the petrol, Monsieur le Maire. Can't you do something? They're bound to ask Madame Soupeau about it.

MAYOR: I don't think we need to worry about Madame Soupeau, Simone.

SIMONE: I could do something. I know my way round the brickworks.

MAYOR *vaguely*: I hope you're not thinking of doing anything rash, Simone. The Commune of Saint-Martin is a great responsibility for me, you know.

SIMONE: Yes, Monsieur le Maire.

MAYOR: I can't think why I'm talking to you like this. You're still a child, Simone. But I think we each of us have to do what we can now, eh?

SIMONE: Yes, Monsieur le Maire. Suppose the brickworks burnt down . . .

MAYOR: For God's sake. You mustn't even think of such a thing. And now I have to go in. This is the hardest path I have ever trodden. *He is about to go in.*

The Capitaine comes out.

CAPITAINE: Monsieur Chavez. You're just in time for breakfast.

MAYOR: I have had it.

CAPITAINE: Pity. You don't seem to have got the picture quite right. Yesterday a number of undesirable incidents occurred here with the connivance of the authorities. It is regrettable that this impudent attempt on the part of certain elements to exploit France's collapse for their own selfish ends was not stamped on at once. Our German guests expect at least a polite gesture from us. For example the German Kommandant has already been told about the stocks in a particular brickworks. You might bear that in mind, Chavez. Perhaps it will improve your appetite. After you, Monsieur le Maire.

MAYOR *very unsure:* After you, mon Capitaine.

They go into the hostelry. Père Gustave comes out of the store and follows them.

PÈRE GUSTAVE *as he carries in a plate of delicacies:* Hope it keeps fine for you, have a good trip. How the moneybags stick together, eh, Georges? They're selling France like they sell their fancy food! *Exit.*

Simone has followed the scene closely. She has sat down.

GEORGES: Simone! What's the matter with you? Simone! *Simone does not reply. Georges shakes her, but suddenly becomes immobile like a statue. During Simone's Daydream which follows, Père Gustave's phrase 'How the moneybags stick together' is quietly and mechanically repeated.*

Daydream of Simone Machard

20 June

Confused martial music. The hostelry's back wall becomes transparent. In front of an immense tapestry sit the Mayor (as King Charles), the Capitaine (Duke of Burgundy), the Hauptmann as the English Commander-in-Chief with his sword across his knees, and Madame Soupeau (the Queen Mother Isabeau) all playing cards at a marble-topped table.

MADAME SOUPEAU: I no longer wish to see that mob, my lord.

HAUPTMANN: Come, hide behind us, Queen Isabeau. I'll have the yard cleared, and then law and order will prevail. Trumped you!

MAYOR: Hark now! Is that a sound of drums I hear?
Joan's drum can be heard in the distance.

CAPITAINE: Play your ace of clubs. I hear nothing.
The drumming stops.

MAYOR: No? I fear, Duke, that my Joan has met with trouble and is in need of help.

CAPITAINE: The ten of hearts. I need peace if I am to sell my wine.

HAUPTMANN: How much is your fancy food, Madame?

MADAME SOUPEAU: Whose deal? Ten thousand pieces of silver, my lord.

MAYOR: But this time I am certain. She is in danger, in mortal danger. I must hasten to her and help her destroy everything. *He gets up holding his cards.*

CAPITAINE: Take care. If you go now it will be the last time. You have not got the picture right. How can one play with all these interruptions? Jack of clubs.

MAYOR *sitting down again:* Very well then.

MADAME SOUPEAU *boxing his ears:* That is for your obstinacy.

HAUPTMANN: Permit me, Queen Isabeau. *He throws some coins on the table, counting:* One, two, three . . .

GEORGES *shaking Simone to wake her from her daydream, while the Hauptmann goes on counting.* Simone! You're dreaming with your eyes wide open.

SIMONE: Are you coming with me, Monsieur Georges?

GEORGES *staring at his bandaged arm; joyfully:* Simone, I can move it again.

SIMONE: That's good. But we must go to the brickworks, Monsieur Georges. We haven't much time. Père Gustave, you must come too. Quickly.

PÈRE GUSTAVE *coming out of the hostelry:* Me? They've put up a poster: 'Saboteurs will be executed.' They're not joking.

SIMONE: The Mayor wishes it.

PÈRE GUSTAVE: The Mayor's a creep.

SIMONE: But you'll come with me, Monsieur Georges? It's for André's sake. I'd never know how to blow up so much petrol. Does one have to set the whole brickworks alight?

GEORGES: Didn't you get it? I can move my arm again.

SIMONE *looking at him:* So neither of you wants to come with me?

PÈRE GUSTAVE: Here's another of them.

A German soldier comes into the yard carrying luggage. As soon as Simone sees him she quickly runs off in fear.

THE GERMAN SOLDIER *throws down the luggage, takes off his steel helmet, wipes his brow and tries amiably to communicate by gestures:* Hauptmann? Inside?

GEORGES *gesticulating:* There. In the hostelry. Cigarette?

THE GERMAN SOLDIER *taking the cigarette and grinning:* War shit. *Imitates the action of shooting, negative gesture.*

GEORGES *laughingly:* Bang bang! *Makes a raspberry; both laugh.*

THE GERMAN SOLDIER: Hauptmann Arsehole.

GEORGES: What? What did you say?

THE GERMAN SOLDIER *mimicking the Hauptmann and his monocle:* Merde.

GEORGES *catches on, and in turn cheerfully mimics the Capitaine and Madame Soupeau:* Merde the lot.

They laugh again, then the German soldier picks up his luggage and goes inside.

GEORGES *to Père Gustave:* O my, O my, how easily we could get on.

PÈRE GUSTAVE: Better be careful.

GEORGES: And how. Now that my arm is mending.

From the hostelry come the Hauptmann, the Capitaine, the Mayor and Madame Soupeau.

CAPITAINE: Herr Hauptmann, I'm delighted we understand one another so well.

HAUPTMANN: Madame, I wish to thank you for volunteering to let us use your petrol. Not that the German army is short. But we accept it as a token of good will and co-operativeness.

MADAME SOUPEAU: It's not far to the brickworks.

HAUPTMANN: I will tell the tanks to go there.

The sky has reddened. The group stands as if petrified. Distant explosions.

HAUPTMANN: What's that?

CAPITAINE *hoarsely:* The brickworks.

(*b*)

It is night. There is a hammering at the gate. Georges comes out of his room and opens up to find the Patron and the two drivers outside.

PATRON: How are things, Georges? Is my mother all right? So the hostelry is still standing. I feel as if I'd been through the Flood. Hullo, Simone.

Simone, scantily dressed, comes from the drivers' quarters. Robert embraces her. Père Gustave has also appeared.

ROBERT: Oh, so you're living in our quarters now? *He dances around with her, humming:*

Joe the strangler came back home

Rosa was still there

And Mama had a chartreuse

And Papa a beer.

PATRON: What's been happening?

GEORGES: A German captain has moved in. Madame Soupeau is a bit tired because of the brickworks inquiry. The
German captain . . .

PATRON: What inquiry?

SIMONE: Monsieur Henri, everything's been done as you
wanted. I took some more food to the hall last night.

PATRON: I'm asking you about the brickworks.

GEORGES *hesitantly*: It burnt down, Monsieur Henri.

PATRON: Burnt down?—The Germans? *Georges shakes his
head.* Carelessness? *Looks from one to the other. No reply.* The
authorities?

GEORGES: No.

PATRON: That scum from the hall.

GEORGES: No, Monsieur Henri.

PATRON: Arson, then. *He wails as if he had caught his foot in a
snare.* Who? *No reply.* Oh, I see, you're all in this together.
In cold fury: So you've taken to crime, how nice. I might
have guessed it after the way you showed your gratitude
my last day here. 'You can stuff your china,' eh, Père
Gustave? Very well then, I accept your challenge. We shall
see.

GEORGES: It happened because of the Germans, Monsieur
Henri.

PATRON *sarcastically:* Oh, I see, it was my brickworks but the
arson was against the Germans. You were so blinded by
hatred, so set on destruction that you bit the hand that fed
you; is that it? *Abruptly:* Simone!

SIMONE: Yes, Monsieur Henri.

PATRON: Now tell me at once who did it.

SIMONE: Me, Monsieur.

PATRON: What? You dared . . . ? *Pulls her by the arm.* Who
told you to? Who was behind it?

SIMONE: Nobody, Monsieur.

PATRON: Don't lie to me, do you hear? I won't stand for . . .

GEORGES: Please leave her alone, Monsieur Henri. She isn't
lying.

PATRON: Who ordered you to?

SIMONE: I did it for my brother.

PATRON: Ah, André! He incited you against your *Patron*, eh? 'Us underdogs', eh? I always knew he was a Red. Who helped you?

SIMONE: Nobody, Monsieur.

PATRON: And why did you do it?

SIMONE: Because of the petrol, Monsieur.

PATRON: And that meant you had to set the entire brick-works alight? Why couldn't you just have let the petrol out?

SIMONE: I didn't know how.

GEORGES: She's a child, Monsieur Henri.

PATRON: Fire-raisers! All of you! Criminals! Get off my property this moment, Père Gustave! Georges, you're fired! You people are worse than the Germans.

GEORGES: Very well, Monsieur Henri. *He walks over and stands beside Simone.*

PATRON: Didn't you say something about an inquiry? What about it?

GEORGES: The Germans are investigating.

PATRON: You mean it happened after the Germans got here?

GEORGES: Yes.

PATRON *sits down in disbelief and desperation:* That's the last straw. It means the hostelry is finished! *Hides his head in his hands.*

PÈRE GUSTAVE: You know, Monsieur Henri, they were saying very good things in Saint-Martin yesterday about the hostelry. 'Right under the Germans' noses', they said.

PATRON: They'll court-martial me. That's what you've done for me. *Desperately:* I'll be shot.

SIMONE *stepping forward:* Monsieur, you'll not be shot, because it was me that did it. Come with me to the German captain and I'll admit everything, Monsieur.

MAURICE: That's out of the question.

PATRON: Why is it out of the question? She's a child. Nobody will touch her.

MAURICE: Tell the Germans it was her if you like, but we'll get her away. Get dressed at once, Simone.

PATRON: That'll make us her accomplices.

SIMONE: Maurice, I must stay. André wants me to, I know it.

PATRON: It all depends whether she did it before the Germans got here or after. If she did it before, it was an act of war and they can't do a thing to her.

PÈRE GUSTAVE *ingratiatingly:* They put up a poster right away saying saboteurs would be shot, Monsieur Henri.

PATRON *to Simone:* Did you see that poster?

SIMONE: Yes, Monsieur Henri.

PATRON: What did it look like?

SIMONE: It was printed on red paper.

PATRON: Is that right? *Père Gustave nods.* Now I'm going to ask the question the Germans will ask you, Simone. Did you read it after you started the fire? If so, then it was not sabotage, Simone, and they can't touch you.

SIMONE: I read it before, Monsieur.

PATRON: You didn't get what I was driving at. If you read it afterwards the Germans will probably just hand you over to the Mayor, because then it was a purely French concern, and that means you'll be out of it, Simone. Do you get that?

SIMONE: Yes, Monsieur. But I read it before.

PATRON: She's confused. Père Gustave, you were in the yard at the time. When did Simone leave?

PÈRE GUSTAVE: Before the poster was put up, of course, Monsieur Henri.

PATRON: There you are.

SIMONE: You're mistaken, Père Gustave. You told me yourself before I left that the poster said I mustn't.

PÈRE GUSTAVE: I told you nothing of the sort.

PATRON: Of course not.

MAURICE: Don't you realize, Monsieur Henri, that the child refuses to join in your monkey tricks? She's not ashamed of what she did.

SIMONE: But the Patron's only trying to help me, Maurice.

PATRON: Exactly. You trust me, don't you, Simone? So listen carefully. It's the enemy we'll be talking to now. That makes all the difference, get me? They'll ask you lots of questions, but you must only answer in a way that's good for Saint-Martin and good for the French. Simple enough, eh?

SIMONE: Yes, Monsieur, but I don't want to say anything that's not right.

PATRON: I understand that. You don't want to say anything that's untrue. Not even to the enemy. Good. I respect that. There's only one thing I would ask you: say nothing, leave it to us. Leave it to me. *Almost in tears:* I'll stand by you through thick and thin, you know that. We'll all stand by you. We are Frenchmen.

SIMONE: Yes, Monsieur.

The Patron takes Simone by the hand and leads her into the hostelry.

MAURICE: She didn't read her book right.

4

THE TRIAL

(*a*)

Fourth Dream of Simone Machard

Night of 21–2 June

A jumble of music. In the courtyard stands the Hauptmann in armour and Simone as Maid of Orleans, surrounded by soldiers in black chain-mail decorated with swastikas; one of whom, identifiable as the Hauptmann's batman, holds a swastika banner.

HAUPTMANN: We've got you now, Joan of Orleans, and you are going to be handed over to a court which will decide why we should condemn you to die at the stake.

Exeunt all except Simone and the standard bearer.

SIMONE: What kind of a court is that?

STANDARD BEARER: Not the ordinary kind. It's ecclesiastical.

SIMONE: I'm admitting nothing.

STANDARD BEARER: That's fine, but the trial seems to be already over.

SIMONE: You mean they sentence you before examining you?

STANDARD BEARER: Of course.

People who have apparently been attending the trial leave the hostelry and cross the yard into the street.

PÈRE GUSTAVE *as he crosses the yard, to Thérèse:* Death! At her age!

THÉRÈSE: Who'd have expected that, even two days back?

SIMONE *pulling her by the sleeve:* Did Hitler come himself?

Thérèse seems not to notice her and leaves with Père Gustave. Simone's parents cross the yard, the father in uniform, the mother in black.

MADAME MACHARD *sobbing:* She was always very obstinate even as a little girl. Just like her brother. It's a terrible blow for Monsieur Machard. Now that he's working for the council, too! What a disgrace! *Both exeunt.*

The brothers Maurice and Robert cross the yard.

ROBERT: She didn't look at all bad.

MAURICE: Especially in that frilly blue dress.

SIMONE *pulling Robert by the sleeve:* Did you see the judges?

ROBERT *casually:* Yes, of course.

SIMONE: Shall I see them too?

ROBERT: Sure to. They'll come out here and sentence you to death. *Exeunt both.*

A LOUD VOICE: Pray silence for the Cardinals and Archbishops of the Ecclesiastical Court of Rouen! Sentence on the Maid of Orleans will now be pronounced. First the staff will be broken over the Maid.

Out of the hostelry steps one of the judges, adorned in magnificent cardinal's robes. He hides his identity behind a breviary, and crosses the yard. He stops behind a bronze tripod with a kettle on it, turns his back, claps the breviary shut, takes a small staff out of his sleeve, solemnly breaks it, and throws the pieces into the kettle.

THE LOUD VOICE: His eminence the Bishop of Beauvais.
For liberating the city of Orleans: death.
Before moving on he looks back indifferently over his shoulder. It is the Colonel.
SIMONE: Monsieur le Colonel!
Another judge steps out of the hostelry and repeats the procedure.
THE LOUD VOICE: For liberating the city of Orleans and for feeding the rats of Orleans with stolen food: death.
The second judge likewise shows his face. It is the Capitaine.
SIMONE: Monsieur le Capitaine!
A third judge steps from the hostelry and repeats the procedure.
THE LOUD VOICE: For launching an attack on the city of Paris and the black market petrol: death.
The third judge is the Patron.
SIMONE: But Monsieur Henri, it's me you're sentencing!
The Patron makes his usual gesture of helplessness, and a fourth judge steps out of the hostelry and repeats the procedure.
THE LOUD VOICE: For uniting all Frenchmen: death.
The fourth judge grips his breviary too convulsively, and drops it. He tries to pick it up quickly, and is recognized: it is the Mayor.
SIMONE: The Mayor himself! Oh, Monsieur Chavez!
THE LOUD VOICE: Your supreme judges have spoken, Joan.
SIMONE: But they're all Frenchmen. *To the standard bearer:* There must be some mistake.
STANDARD BEARER: No, Mademoiselle, this is a French court.
The four judges have stopped at the entrance to the yard.
MAYOR: You must know that from your book. Of course the Maid is sentenced by French judges, and rightly so since she is French.
SIMONE *confused:* That's true. I know from the book that I'll be sentenced to death. But I would like to know why. I never really understood that part.
MAYOR *to the judges:* She is asking for a trial.
CAPITAINE: What would be the point of that as she's already been sentenced?

MAYOR: Well, at least the case would have been examined, the defendant interrogated, and everything discussed and weighed up.

COLONEL: And found inadequate. *Shrugging his shoulders:* But very well then, if *you* insist on it.

PATRON: We're not prepared, you know.

They put their heads together and confer in whispers. Père Gustave carries out a table and puts plates and candles on it. The judges sit down at it.

PÈRE GUSTAVE: The refugees from the hall are outside. They're asking to be admitted to the trial.

PATRON: Out of the question. I'm expecting my mother, and she doesn't like the way they smell.

CAPITAINE *calling into the background:* The trial will be held in camera. In the interests of the state.

PATRON: Where are the papers? Probably gone astray again, like everything else in this country.

MAYOR: Where is the plaintiff?

The judges look at each other.

MAYOR: Without a plaintiff it can't be official.

PATRON: Père Gustave, go and get us a plaintiff from the store room.

PÈRE GUSTAVE *calls from the gate towards the street:* The High Ecclesiastical Court of Rouen calls on anybody who has a complaint to bring against the Maid.—Nobody? *He repeats his challenge. Then to the judges:* Here comes the plaintiff: Isabeau the Queen Mother, supporter of the treacherous Duke of Burgundy and of the hereditary enemy.

MADAME SOUPEAU *in armour comes out of the hostelry and greets the judges, who bow low before her. With the routine amiability of a great hôtelière:* Good evening, mon Capitaine. Don't get up. Don't let me disturb you. *Over her shoulder into the hostelry:* One portion of Alsace-Lorraine for Monsieur le Capitaine, well done! How would you like your peasants, Connétable? I hope you are satisfied with the service this time, mon Colonel. *Pointing to Simone:* Everything would have been saved if this Maid of Orleans hadn't interfered in

the negotiations. Everything: France and the brickworks
too. You are too weak, gentlemen. Who makes the decisions here, the Church or a servant from the hostelry?
Starts shouting like one possessed: I demand and insist that this
person be put to death immediately for heresy and dis-
obedience, not to say obstinacy. Heads must roll. Blood
must flow. She must be bloodily exterminated. She must
serve as a bloody example. *Exhausted:* My smelling-salts.

CAPITAINE: A chair for the Queen Mother.

Père Gustave brings her a chair.

PATRON: Isn't your armour rather tight, Maman? Why are
you wearing it, anyhow?

MADAME SOUPEAU: Well, I'm at war too, aren't I?

PATRON: At war? What war?

MADAME SOUPEAU: My war. Against this rebellious Maid
who has been stirring up the people in the village hall.

CAPITAINE *sharply:* Shh! *To Simone:* What right had you to
lead the French to war, Maid?

SIMONE: An angel told me to, venerable Bishop of Beauvais.
The judges look at each other.

PATRON: I see, an angel. What sort of an angel?

SIMONE: From the church. The one to the left of the altar.

CAPITAINE: Never set eyes on him.

MAYOR *friendlily:* What did this angel look like? Describe
him.

SIMONE: He was very young and had a beautiful voice,
honourable sirs. He told me I must . . .

COLONEL *interrupting:* What he told you is of no interest to
us. What sort of an accent did he have? Was it an educated
one? Or the other kind?

SIMONE: I don't know. He just spoke.

CAPITAINE: Aha.

PATRON: What sort of clothes did this angel wear?

SIMONE: He was beautifully dressed. His robe was made of
stuff you'd pay twenty or thirty francs a yard for in Tours.

CAPITAINE: Do I understand you correctly, Simone or
Joan, as the case may be? So he wasn't one of those great

magnificent angels whose robes cost perhaps as much as two or three hundred francs a yard?

SIMONE: I don't know.

COLONEL: What condition was the robe in? Quite worn?

SIMONE: The angel was just a bit chipped, around the sleeve.

COLONEL: I see. Chipped around the sleeve. As if he'd had to wear it to work too? Was it torn?

SIMONE: No, not torn.

CAPITAINE: All the same, it was chipped. And at the place where it had been chipped, the sleeve could quite well have got torn with all that work. Perhaps the reason why you didn't see it was that it was exactly where the colour had rubbed off. But it could have been, couldn't it? *Simone does not reply.*

COLONEL: Did the angel say anything that a person of quality might have said? Think that over.

SIMONE: General things, mostly.

MAYOR: Did the angel resemble anyone you knew?

SIMONE *quietly:* My brother André.

COLONEL: Ah, a private soldier. Private Machard. Gentlemen, now it's out. A most peculiar angel, I must say.

MADAME SOUPEAU: A real public-bar angel, a gutter seraph! In any case now we know where those 'Voices' come from. From the taverns and the sewage farms.

SIMONE: You shouldn't run down the angel, Reverend Sirs.

PATRON: If you look on page 124 of your book you will see that we are the Ecclesiastical Court, in fact the highest authority on earth.

COLONEL: Don't you think that we, the high Cardinals of France, know the will of God better than some jumped-up angel?

CAPITAINE: Where does God dwell, Joan? Below or above? And where did your so-called angel come from? From below. So who sent him? God? Or could it have been the Devil?

MADAME SOUPEAU: The Devil! Joan of Orleans, the voices you heard came from the Devil.

SIMONE *strongly:* No, no! Not from the Devil!

CAPITAINE: Call him, call your angel! Perhaps he'll defend you, great Maid of Orleans. Usher, do your duty.

PÈRE GUSTAVE *calls:* The Supreme Ecclesiastical Court of Rouen calls upon the angel, name unknown, who, so the Maid alleges, has appeared to her on several occasions, to come and bear witness on her behalf.

Simone looks at the garage roof. It remains empty. Père Gustave repeats his summons. Simone, in great anguish, looks at the smiling judges. Then she crouches down and in her confusion begins to drum on the ground. However, there is no sound and the garage roof remains empty.

SIMONE: It does not resound here. What has happened? It doesn't resound. French soil no longer resounds. It doesn't resound here.

MADAME SOUPEAU *stepping towards her:* Are you in the least aware who *is* France?

(*b*)

Morning of 22 June. Over the gate the French flag is at half-mast and is swathed in black ribbon. Georges, Robert and Père Gustave are listening to Maurice as he reads to them from a black-bordered newspaper.

MAURICE: The Marshal says the honour of France is not impaired by the armistice terms.

PÈRE GUSTAVE: That's a great comfort to me.

MAURICE: Me too. The Marshal goes on to say that a new order and discipline are needed and that the French people must gather round him and look to him as a father.

PÈRE GUSTAVE: That's it. André has stopped fighting, they've laid down their arms. Now he has got to be brought under strict discipline.

GEORGES: Good thing Simone's no longer here.

From the hostelry comes the Hauptmann, bareheaded and beltless, smoking an after-breakfast cigar. He gives them an indifferent

*glance, strolls to the gate, briefly looks up the street and returns at a
quickened pace into the hostelry.*

PÈRE GUSTAVE: He never liked having a child mixed up in
this.

GEORGES: I'm surprised at her running away, I really am.
She always said she'd stay whatever happened. Something
must have scared her. She simply disappeared through the
laundry-room window.

Enter the Patron from the hostelry, rubbing his hands.

PATRON: Maurice, Robert! Go and unload the crates with the
china and silver! *Looking round, then quietly:* I'm not going to
ask if any of you helped a certain person to get away last
night. What's past is past, and I don't mind telling you it's
the best thing that could have happened in the circumstances. Not that there was any real danger. The Germans
are not cannibals. Besides, your *Patron* knows how to talk
to them. As I told the German captain at breakfast, 'What's
the point of it all? Before reading the notice, or after reading
the notice! It's a farce. A child: what do you expect? A
little soft in the head perhaps, a bit psycho . . . Tanks! Right,
stop them, destroy everything! And playing with matches
of course is always good fun. A political act? More like a
childish prank!'

GEORGES *looking at the others:* A childish prank? What do you
mean by that, Monsieur Henri?

PATRON: I said the same thing to my mother: she's a child,
I said.

GEORGES: That child was the only person in the hostelry that
did her duty. Nobody else lifted a finger. And the people of
Saint-Martin won't forget it, Monsieur Henri.

PATRON *irritably:* Why don't you people get on with *your*
duty? Get those crates unloaded. I'm only glad it's all over.
I'm sure the Herr Hauptmann won't spend much more
time looking for Simone. And now get on with the job!
That's what our poor France needs now! *Exit.*

GEORGES: She's gone: great relief all round.

MAURICE: And it had nothing at all to do with patriotism or

anything of that sort. That would have been awkward. 'The Germans are not cannibals.' Just as we were about to make a fine gesture and hand the Germans the petrol we'd been withholding from our own army, along comes the mob and starts getting all patriotic.

Through the gateway comes the Mayor. He looks pale and does not acknowledge their greetings as he goes into the hostelry.

MAYOR *turning round:* Are there sentries outside Madame Soupeau's door?

PÈRE GUSTAVE: No, Monsieur Chavez.

Exit the Mayor.

PÈRE GUSTAVE: He's probably here because the Germans want the village hall cleared. Unless it was Madame Soupeau who wanted it.

ROBERT: Their new order and discipline!

PÈRE GUSTAVE: About Simone, Maurice: they had to treat it as an ordinary case of arson if the insurance company was to make the damage good. Trust them not to miss a trick.

Simone is marched through the gate flanked by two German soldiers with fixed bayonets.

GEORGES: Simone! What's happened?

SIMONE *stops, very pale:* I was down at the hall.

ROBERT: Don't be afraid. The Germans won't do anything to you.

SIMONE: Last night when they interrogated me, Robert, they said I'd be handed over to the French authorities.

GEORGES: Why did you run away?

Simone does not reply. The soldiers push her into the hostelry.

MAURICE: So the Germans don't consider the matter finished. Monsieur Henri's wrong.

Monsieur and Madame Machard come through the gate, the former in his municipal uniform.

MADAME MACHARD: Have they brought her in already? That's terrible. Monsieur Machard is quite beside himself. It's not just that our rent is due. What really upsets Monsieur Machard is the disgrace. I always knew it would end like this; all that reading of hers has turned her head. At seven this morning there was a knock on the door, and there were the Germans outside. 'Messieurs,' I said, 'if you can't find our daughter then she must have done something desperate. Arson or no, nothing would have made her leave the hostelry. She'd have stayed for her brother's sake if for nothing else.'

Enter the Patron from the hostelry.

PATRON: It's more than I can take, Madame Machard! She's cost me 100,000 francs. How much she's cost in wear and tear to my nerves I couldn't say.

Enter Madame Soupeau from the hostelry. She holds Simone tightly by the arm and drags the reluctant girl to the store room. Behind them the Mayor and Capitaine Fétain. The four go into the store. The others watch in amazement.

MAYOR *standing at the door of the store room:* Machard, run across to the hall and see the evacuation goes off all right. Tell them the Germans need the space. *Exit into the store.*

MADAME MACHARD: Very good, Monsieur le Maire. *Both Machards stalk off with dignity.*

ROBERT: What do they want her in the store room for? What's going to happen to her, Monsieur Henri?

PATRON: Don't ask so many questions. We're carrying an immense responsibility. One wrong step and the hostelry is ruined.

MADAME SOUPEAU: Monsieur le Maire, I think I've demonstrated to you by the evidence of your own eyes that she left the cellar unlocked with provisions in it including 50,000 francs' worth of rare wines. How many crates have disappeared I can only guess. She deliberately deceived me by returning the key to me in your presence. *To Simone:* Simone, I was told that you yourself carried whole baskets full of food to the village hall. How much did they pay you? Where is the money?

SIMONE: I didn't take money, Madame.

MADAME SOUPEAU: Don't lie to me. And another thing: the morning when Monsieur Henri left he was threatened by the mob because a rumour was going about that the lorries were to be taken away. Was it you who put about that rumour?

SIMONE: I told Monsieur le Maire, Madame.

MADAME SOUPEAU: Who else was in the Mayor's office when you told him? Refugees?

SIMONE: Yes, I think so.

MADAME SOUPEAU: Oh, you think so. Then when the mob arrived, what did you tell them to do with the food stores of the hostelry where you were working? *Simone does not understand.* Did you or did you not tell them to help themselves to whatever they wanted?

SIMONE: I can't remember, Madame.

MADAME SOUPEAU: So . . .

MAYOR: What are you getting at, Madame?

MADAME SOUPEAU: Who were the first people to help themselves, Simone? Exactly: your parents. And they didn't do too badly.

ROBERT: That's the limit. *To Madame Soupeau:* It was you yourself pushed all those tins on to the Machards.

GEORGES *simultaneously:* It was you yourself told the Mayor to dispose of the stores as he saw fit.

MAYOR: Quite so, Madame.

MADAME SOUPEAU *ignoring the last remarks, to Simone:* You were impudent, disloyal and obstinate. That's why I dismissed you. Did you leave immediately, as I told you?

SIMONE: No, Madame.

MADAME SOUPEAU: Instead, you hung around here and then tried to get your own back for being dismissed by setting the brickworks on fire. Correct?

SIMONE *defiantly:* I did it because of the Germans.

ROBERT: Everyone in Saint-Martin knows that.

MADAME SOUPEAU: Oh, I see: because of the Germans. How did you know the Germans would discover the petrol?

SIMONE: I heard Monsieur le Capitaine talking about it to Monsieur le Maire.

MADAME SOUPEAU: Ah, so you heard we were intending to report the petrol?

SIMONE: Monsieur le Capitaine was intending to.

MADAME SOUPEAU: So your only reason for destroying the petrol was to stop us handing it over? That's just what I wanted to hear.

SIMONE *desperately:* I did it because of the enemy! There were those three tanks outside the Mairie.

MADAME SOUPEAU: And that was the enemy? Or was it somebody else? *Two nuns appear in the gateway escorted by a policeman.*

MAYOR: What is it, Jules?

POLICEMAN: These ladies are sisters of the Disciplinary Order of Saint Ursula.

CAPITAINE: I phoned the convent in your name, Chavez. *To the nuns:* This is the Machard girl, sisters.

MAYOR: How dare you?

CAPITAINE: You're surely not thinking of letting her go free, Monsieur Chavez? *Menacingly:* The least our guests can expect is that we cleanse Saint-Martin of all dangerous elements. I don't think you've fully understood our venerable Marshal's speech. France is faced with a period of danger. Insubordination is contagious, and it's up to us to nip it in the bud. One such fire in Saint-Martin is more than enough, Chavez.

MAURICE: Ah, so now it's up to us to do the Germans' dirty work for them. And it looks as if we're only too glad to.

MADAME SOUPEAU *coldly:* Of course I shall get the Public Prosecutor in Tours to authorize the girl's formal commitment. The brickworks are property of the hostelry, and Simone set fire to them from base personal motives.

GEORGES: Personal motives indeed, with Simone!

MAYOR *quite shaken:* Are you determined to destroy the child?

ROBERT *menacingly:* Who's getting her own back now?

PATRON: Don't start in again, Robert. As she's under age she'll be in the care of the Sisters, that's all.

MAURICE *horrified:* At Saint Ursula's, where they flog them!

SIMONE *screaming:* No!

MAYOR: Simone to go to that institution for the mentally

retarded? That mental torture-house, that hell? Do you
realize you're condemning her to madness?

MAURICE *pointing to the figures of the brutish nuns:* Just look at
them.

*The nuns do not stir a muscle. Their faces remain cold and mask-
like.*

GEORGES: It would have been more merciful to let the Germans execute her.

SIMONE *begging for help:* That's where they finish with their
heads swollen up and spit running out of their mouths,
Monsieur le Maire. They chain them up!

MAYOR *firmly:* Madame Soupeau, I shall testify at the inquiry
in Tours as to the true motives of this child. Be calm,
Simone, everybody knows you only acted out of patriotism.

MADAME SOUPEAU *in an outburst:* Ah, so our little pétroleuse
is to be a national heroine and a saint, is that the idea?
France is saved: France is on fire. On my right the German
tanks, on my left Simone Machard the day-labourer's
daughter.

CAPITAINE: My dear Monsieur Chavez, with a past like
yours the judges of the New France aren't likely to give
much weight to your testimony. Besides, the road to Tours
has become a little unsafe for people like you.

MAURICE *with bitterness:* You see what they're up to: defending Saint-Martin against any suggestion that there might be
Frenchmen here.

MADAME SOUPEAU: Frenchmen? *Gets hold of Simone, shakes
her:* Are you trying to teach us how to be patriotic? The
Soupeaus have owned this hostelry for two hundred years.
To everybody: Do you want to see a patriot? *Pointing to the
Capitaine:* There's one for you. We're perfectly capable of
telling you when there must be war and when peace is
better. You want to do something for France? Right. *We*
are France, do you get that?

CAPITAINE: You're getting too worked up, Marie. Once and
for all, Monsieur le Maire, tell them to remove the Machard
girl.

MAYOR: Me? *You* seem to have taken charge here now. *Turns away as if to leave.*

SIMONE *afraid:* Don't go, Monsieur le Maire!

MAYOR *helplessly:* Keep your chin up, Simone! *Stumbles away, a broken man.*

MADAME SOUPEAU *after a silence, to the Capitaine:* Get this scandalous business finished, Honoré!

CAPITAINE *to the policeman:* I'll take the responsibility. *The policeman gets hold of Simone.*

SIMONE *in a whisper, extremely frightened:* Not to Saint Ursula's!

ROBERT: You bastard! *Tries to attack the policeman.*

MAURICE *holding him back:* Don't be a fool, Robert. There's nothing we can do for her now. They've got the police and they've got the Germans. Poor Simone, too many enemies.

MADAME SOUPEAU: Simone, fetch your things.
Simone looks around, her friends are silent and cast their glances downwards. She goes into the store room in great anguish.

MADAME SOUPEAU *calmly, half to her employees, in explanation:* The child is insubordinate and won't acknowledge any kind of authority. It is our painful duty to teach order and discipline to her.
Simone returns with a tiny suitcase, carrying her apron over her arm. She hands the apron to Madame Soupeau.

MADAME SOUPEAU: And now open your suitcase so that we can see what you are taking with you.

PATRON: Is that really necessary, Maman?
One of the nuns has already opened the suitcase. She takes out Simone's book.

SIMONE: Not the book!
The nun hands the book over to Madame Soupeau.

MADAME SOUPEAU: This is the hostelry's property.

PATRON: I gave it to her.

MADAME SOUPEAU: It didn't do her much good. *To Simone:* Simone, say goodbye to the staff.

SIMONE: Goodbye, Monsieur Georges.

GEORGES: Will you be brave, Simone?

SIMONE: Yes, Monsieur Georges.

MAURICE: Keep well.

SIMONE: Yes, Maurice.

GEORGES: I shan't forget your cousin.

Simone smiles at him. She looks up at the garage roof. The light dims. Music commences, announcing the appearance of the angel. Simone looks towards the garage roof and sees him there.

THE ANGEL

France's daughter, don't be afraid.

No one can live long by fighting the Maid.

Each hand lifted to do you harm

Soon must wither away on its arm.

No matter where they may send you to

France will always go with you.

And before much time has passed

Glorious she will rise at last.

The angel disappears, full light returns. The nuns grip Simone by the arm. Simone kisses Maurice and Robert, then is led away. Everybody watches in silence.

SIMONE *at the gate, struggling desperately:* No, no! I won't go! Help me, can't you! Not to that place! André! André!
She is dragged away.

MADAME SOUPEAU: My smelling-salts, Henri.

PATRON *gloomily:* Maurice, Robert, Georges, Père Gustave, get cracking! Don't forget it's peacetime now.
The Patron and the Capitaine take Madame Soupeau into the hostelry. Maurice and Robert leave by the gate. Père Gustave rolls a tyre into the yard to mend it. Georges examines his bad arm. The sky begins to redden. Père Gustave points at it and shows Georges. The Patron dashes out of the hostelry.

PATRON: Maurice, Robert! Go at once and find out what's burning!

PÈRE GUSTAVE: It must be the village hall. Those refugees! They seem to have learned something.

GEORGES: They can't have got to Saint Ursula's yet. Simone will see the fire from the car.

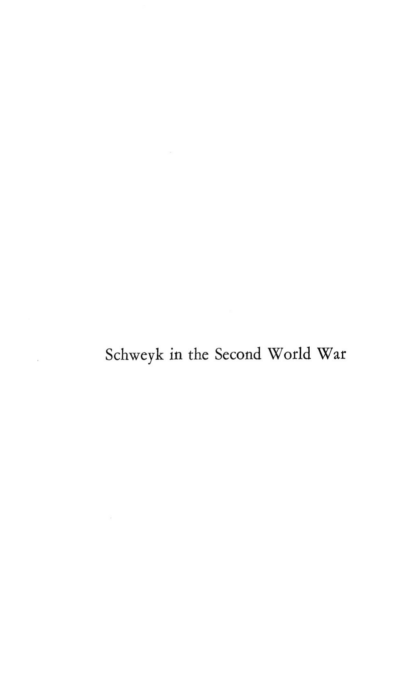

Schweyk in the Second World War

Translator: WILLIAM ROWLINSON

Characters

Schweyk, dog dealer in Prague · Baloun, a photographer, his friend · Anna Kopecka, landlady of the Chalice tavern · Young Prochazka, son of a butcher, her admirer · Anna, a servant girl · Kati, her friend

Brettschneider, Gestapo agent · Bullinger, lieutenant in the SS · SS-man Müller II · The Chaplain

Hitler · Himmler · Goering · Goebbels · von Bock · Minor characters

Martial music. Hitler, Goering, Goebbels and Himmler around a globe. All larger than life except Goebbels, who is smaller than life.

HITLER

Comrades and party members, you've seen how my iron hand

Is holding down Germany, just as we planned.

So here's my chance to bid for world domination

Which is nothing but a small matter of tanks, stukas and determination.

He puts his hand on the globe, and blood slowly spreads across the world. Goering, Goebbels and Himmler shout 'Heil!'

First, though (this is something which even I cannot guess)

Tell me, since you're the head of my police and SS

How would you say the Little Man views me?

Not just the Germans only

But those people in Austria, Czecho-what's-its-name

(What the hell are those small countries called, on my map they all look the same)

Do they support me and—love me indeed?

Can I count on them in a crisis, or are they—more of a broken reed?

What's their view of me, the statesman, orator, warrior, artist—

Just what do they think I am?

HIMMLER

The smartest.

HITLER

And are they truly generous, even to obsession

Specially with their possessions

Which I've got to have for my war, since although I find

I'm quite smart, I'm still only human.

HIMMLER

Not to my mind.

HITLER

Don't interrupt me. But oh, my poor head
Aches as I lie tossing and turning in my bed
Thinking of Europe, wondering how does the Little Man
    view me?

HIMMLER

Mein Führer, they pray to you on bended knee
As to a god, all the while
Loving you as men love a mistress: the same as the Ger-
    mans!

GOERING, GOEBBELS, HIMMLER:

Heil!

I

*In the Chalice tavern sit Schweyk and Baloun over their morning drink.
The landlady, Mrs Anna Kopecka, is serving a drunken SS man. At
the bar sits young Prochazka.*

MRS KOPECKA: You've had five Pilseners, and I'd rather you
    didn't have a sixth. You're not used to it.

SS MAN: Give me another, that's an order. You know what
    that means, and if you're a good girl and do as you're told
    I'll let you into the big secret, you won't be sorry.

MRS KOPECKA: I don't want to know. That's why you're
    not getting any more beer, so you don't let our your secrets
    and make trouble for me.

SS MAN: That's very sensible of you, just what I might have
    recommended myself. All personnel with knowledge of this
    secret will be shot. They've made an attempt on Adolf's
    life, in Munich. He nearly had it: skin of his teeth.

MRS KOPECKA: Shut up, you're drunk.

SCHWEYK *cordially, from the next table:* Which Adolf would
    that be? I know two Adolfs. One of them was behind the
    counter at Prusha the chemist's—he's in a concentration

camp now because he'd only sell his concentrated hydro-
chloric acid to Czechs—and the other's Adolf Kokoschka
who picks up the dogshit and he's in a concentration camp
too for saying there's no shit to beat a British bulldog's.
Neither would be much loss.

SS MAN *gets up and salutes:* Heil Hitler!

SCHWEYK *likewise gets up and salutes:* Heil Hitler!

SS MAN *threateningly:* Anything wrong with that?

SCHWEYK: Present and correct, Mr SS, sir, nothing wrong at
all.

MRS KOPECKA *coming with beer:* Here's your Pilsener, I don't
suppose it makes any difference now. Now just you sit
down nice and quiet and don't start pouring out any more
of your Führer's secrets that none of us wants to hear. We
don't have any politics in this place. *She points to a notice:*
'*Just drink your slivovitz or beer / And don't talk politics in
here. Anna Kopecka*'. I'm running a business. When somebody comes and orders a beer I draw him one, but that's
all.

YOUNG PROCHAZKA *when she returns to the bar:* Why won't
you let people enjoy themselves, Mrs K?

MRS KOPECKA: Because the Nazis'll shut the Chalice down
if I do.

SCHWEYK: If it was Hitler they had a go at it wouldn't half be
a lark.

MRS KOPECKA: You be quiet too, Mr Schweyk. It's nothing
to do with you.

SCHWEYK: If that was it, it could be because there's a shortage
of potatoes. That's the sort of thing people won't put up
with. But it's all on account of order, good order and military
discipline; they've got things that organized every blessed
bunch of parsley is a coupon on your ration card, that's
order for you, and I've heard as how Hitler has put more
things in order than you'd have thought humanly possible.
Once there's no shortage you don't get order. Take me for
instance, suppose I've been and sold a dachshund, there I
am with a pocketful of money, notes and silver all jumbled

up, but when I'm broke there's probably nothing but a one-crown note and a ten-heller piece, and that doesn't leave you much room for disorder. When Mussolini took over in Italy the trains started running on time. They've had seven or eight goes at him so far.

MRS KOPECKA: Stop drivelling and drink your beer. If something's happened we'll all be for it.

SCHWEYK: I don't see why you have to look so miserable about it, Baloun, you'll be odd man out in Prague today.

BALOUN: It's easy enough to say food gets short in a war like this, but I haven't had a real meal since Whit Sunday last year, what with all your ration cards and two ounces of meat a week. *Indicating the SS man:* It's all right for them, look how well fed they are, I'll just go and have a quick word with him. *He goes over to the SS man.* What did you have for lunch, eh, pal, that's made you so thirsty? I hope you don't mind me asking, but I bet it was something pretty hot, goulash perhaps?

SS MAN: Mind your own business, it's a military secret, rissoles.

BALOUN: With gravy. And were there any fresh vegetables? I don't want you to say anything you shouldn't, but just supposing there was cabbage, was there plenty of butter on it? That's the important thing, you know. I remember in Przlov, before Hitler (if you'll pardon my saying so) I had a rissole at the Old Swan that was better than you get at the Ritz.

MRS KOPECKA *to Schweyk:* Can't you get Mr Baloun away from that SS man, yesterday he spent so long asking Mr Brettschneider from the Gestapo—I wonder where's he got to today—about the size of the helpings in the German army, he nearly got himself arrested as a spy.

SCHWEYK: Can't be helped. Eating's his vice.

BALOUN *to the SS man:* D'you happen to know if the Germans are taking on volunteers in Prague for the Russian campaign, and if they get the same size helpings as the German army, or is it just a rumour?

MRS KOPECKA: Mr Baloun, stop bothering that gentleman, he's off duty, and you ought to be ashamed asking such questions, and you a Czech.

BALOUN *guiltily:* I don't mean any harm—I wouldn't go asking him right out like this if I did. I know your point of view, Mrs Kopecka.

MRS KOPECKA: I don't have a point of view, I have a pub. I just expect normal decent behaviour from the customers, but you're terrible, Mr Baloun, you really are.

SS MAN: Do you want to volunteer?

BALOUN: I was only asking.

SS MAN: If you're interested I'll take you along to the recruiting office. The catering's first class, if you want to know. The Ukraine is becoming the granary of the Third Reich. When we were in Holland I sent so many food parcels home I even kept my aunt in grub, and I can't stand the sight of her. Heitler!

BALOUN *also standing up:* Heil Hitler.

SCHWEYK *who has joined them:* You mustn't say 'Heil Hitler', you must do like this gentleman, and he ought to know, say 'Heitler', that shows you're used to it and say it in your sleep at home.

MRS KOPECKA *bringing the SS man a slivovitz:* Have this one on the house.

SS MAN *embracing Baloun:* So you want to volunteer against the Bolsheviks, that's what I like to hear; you may be a Czech pig but you've got brains, I'll come along to the recruiting office with you.

MRS KOPECKA *pushing him down on to his chair:* Drink your slivovitz, it'll calm you down. *To Baloun:* I've half a mind to throw you out. You've no sense of dignity left, it comes from that unnatural gluttony of yours. Do you know that song they're all singing now? I'll sing it to you, you've only had a couple of beers, you should have your senses about you still. *She sings 'The Song of the Nazi Soldier's Wife':*

What did the post bring the soldier's wife
From the ancient city of Prague?
From Prague it brought her some high-heeled shoes.
Just a card with news and some high-heeled shoes
That was what she got from ancient Prague.

What did the post bring the soldier's wife
From Warsaw on Poland's plains?
From Warsaw it brought her a fine linen blouse
To wear in the house, a superb linen blouse.
That was what came from Poland's plains.

What did the post bring the soldier's wife
From Oslo's well-equipped stores?
From Oslo it brought her an elegant fur.
Just the thing for her, an elegant fur!
That was what she got from Oslo's stores.

What did the post bring the soldier's wife
From the port of Rotterdam?
From Rotterdam it brought her a hat.
And she looked good in that very Dutch-looking hat
Which was sent her from Rotterdam.

What did the post bring the soldier's wife
From Brussels in Belgium's fair land?
From Brussels it brought her some delicate laces.
Nothing quite replaces such delicate laces.
That was what she got from Belgium's fair land.

What did the post bring the soldier's wife
From the lights of gay Paree?
From Paree it brought her a lovely silk dress.
To her neighbour's distress, a lovely silk dress
That was what she got from gay Paree.

What did the post bring the soldier's wife
From the desert around Tobruk?
From round Tobruk it brought her a pendant.
A copper pendant that looked so resplendent
That was what it brought her from Tobruk.

What did the post bring the soldier's wife
From the Russian steppe-lands?
From Russia it brought her her widow's veil.
So we end our tale with the widow's veil
Which she got from Russia's steppes.

The SS man nods in triumph at the end of each verse, but before the last his head sinks to the table—he is out to the wide.

SCHWEYK: A very nice song. *To Baloun:* It shows you should think twice before you do anything without thinking. Don't get the idea of going off to Russia with Hitler for the sake of the extra rations, and then freezing to death, you dope.

BALOUN *deeply affected by the song, has propped his head on his elbows and begun to sob:* Mother of God, what's going to become of me the way I am about food? You lot'll have to take me in hand, otherwise I'll go to pieces completely. I can't stay a good Czech on an empty stomach.

SCHWEYK: If you swore by the Virgin Mary never to volunteer out of greed, you'd keep to it. *To Mrs Kopecka:* He's religious. Would you swear, though? No.

BALOUN: I'm not swearing on an empty stomach, it's not funny.

MRS KOPECKA: It's dreadful. You're a grown man, after all.

BALOUN: Yes, but I'm weak.

SCHWEYK: If they put a plate of pork in front of you and said 'Eat, you sinner, but swear you'll stay a good Czech', you'd swear if I know you; I mean, if they kept their hands on the plate and pulled it back straightaway if you didn't swear, you'd swear then all right.

BALOUN: That's true, but they'd have to keep their hands on it.

SCHWEYK: And you'd only keep your word if you knelt down and swore on the Bible and in front of everybody, right? *Baloun nods.*

MRS KOPECKA: It's almost worth a try. *Goes back to young Prochazka.*

YOUNG PROCHAZKA: Soon as you start singing I have to hold myself back.

MRS KOPECKA *absently:* Why?

YOUNG PROCHAZKA: Love.

MRS KOPECKA: How d'you know it's love and not just a passing fancy?

YOUNG PROCHAZKA: I know, Mrs K. Yesterday I wrapped up a customer's handbag for her instead of her cutlet, and got told off by my father, and all because I was thinking of you. And I get headaches first thing in the morning. It's love all right.

MRS KOPECKA: Suppose it is, the question then is how much love.

YOUNG PROCHAZKA: What d'you mean by that, Mrs K?

MRS KOPECKA: I mean, how far is your love prepared to go? Perhaps only spitting distance, I know that kind of love.

YOUNG PROCHAZKA: Mrs K., you cut me to the quick, you really do, with accusations like that. There's no truth in them at all. My love's prepared to go to any lengths if only you'd accept it. But you won't.

MRS KOPECKA: I was wondering for instance whether it would stretch to two pounds of pickled pork.

YOUNG PROCHAZKA: Mrs K! How can you be so materialistic at a moment like this?

MRS KOPECKA *turning away to count bottles:* There you are. Even that's too much.

YOUNG PROCHAZKA *shaking his head:* There you go again. I just don't understand you. Ships that pass in the night, Mrs K.

BALOUN *despairingly:* It didn't only start with the war, it's an old story, this gluttony of mine. It made my sister I used to live with take her kids and go to the saint's festival at Klokota. But even Klokota didn't work. My sister brought the kids back and began to count the hens as soon as she got in. There were one or two missing. I couldn't help it, I knew they were needed for the eggs, but out I went to have a good look at them, suddenly I get this great yawning chasm in my stomach, and an hour later I'm feeling better again and the hen's already plucked. I'm probably beyond help.

YOUNG PROCHAZKA: Did you mean that seriously?

MRS KOPECKA: Quite seriously.

YOUNG PROCHAZKA: Mrs K., when do you want the meat? Tomorrow?

MRS KOPECKA: You're sure you know what you're doing, promising it? You'd have to get it out of your father's shop without his permission and without meat coupons, and that's black-marketeering and you'll be shot if it's found out.

YOUNG PROCHAZKA: Don't you think I would get myself shot for you if I knew it would do me any good?

Schweyk and Baloun have been following the conversation.

SCHWEYK *appreciatively:* Now that's the way a lover ought to be. In Pilsen there was a young man in love with a widow, she wasn't so young, neither, and he hanged himself from a rafter in the barn because she happened to say that he never did anything for her; and down at the Bear a chap cut his wrist open in the gents because the barmaid had given another customer better measure, and him a family man too. A few days later a couple of fellows jumped into the Moldau off the Charles Bridge because of a woman, but that was on account of her money, she was supposed to be well off.

MRS KOPECKA: I must admit a woman doesn't hear that sort of thing every day, Mr Prochazka.

YOUNG PROCHAZKA: She doesn't indeed. I'll bring it to-morrow dinnertime; is that soon enough?

MRS KOPECKA: I don't want you to get yourself into trouble, but it's in a good cause, it's not for me. You heard yourself that Mr Baloun must have a proper meal with meat, or else he gets evil ideas.

YOUNG PROCHAZKA: So you don't want me to get myself into trouble. That just slipped out, sort of, didn't it? So it isn't all the same to you whether I get shot or not, now don't take it back, when you've made me happy. Mrs K., it's settled, you can count on that pickled pork if I have to swing for it.

MRS KOPECKA: Come in tomorrow dinnertime, Mr Baloun, I'm not promising anything, but it looks as if you'll be getting your meal.

BALOUN: If I only get one decent meal I'll get all the evil ideas out of my system. But I'm not going to start counting my chickens till I can stick a fork into 'em. I've been through too much.

SCHWEYK *pointing to the SS man:* I bet he'll have forgotten all about it when he wakes up, he's out to the wide. *Shouts in his ear:* Hurrah for Beneš! *When the SS man doesn't stir:* That's the surest sign that he's unconscious, otherwise he'd have made mincemeat of me, you see that's what they're scared of.

Brettschneider the Gestapo agent has come in.

BRETTSCHNEIDER: Who's scared?

SCHWEYK *firmly:* The SS. Won't you join us, Mr Brettschneider? A Pilsener for the gentleman, Mrs Kopecka, it's a warm day.

BRETTSCHNEIDER: And what are they scared of, in your opinion?

SCHWEYK: Of being caught off their guard and letting slip some treasonable remark, or something like that, I don't know. But perhaps you want to get on with reading your newspaper, don't let me disturb you.

BRETTSCHNEIDER: Nobody ever disturbs me if he has something interesting to say. Mrs Kopecka, you look as fresh as the flowers in May.

MRS KOPECKA *giving him his beer:* September's more like it.

YOUNG PROCHAZKA *when she is back at the bar:* If I were in your place I wouldn't let him take that sort of liberty.

BRETTSCHNEIDER *unfolding his paper:* This is a special edition. There's been an attempt to assassinate the Führer in a Munich beercellar. What do you say to that?

SCHWEYK: Did he suffer long?

BRETTSCHNEIDER: He wasn't harmed, the bomb went off too late.

SCHWEYK: Probably a cheap one. Everything's mass-produced these days, and then people are surprised when they don't get the quality stuff. Stands to reason something like that can't be made with the same loving care like when they were hand-done, I mean, doesn't it? But I must say they were a bit careless not to pick a better bomb for a job like that. There used to be a butcher in Cesky Krumlov who . . .

BRETTSCHNEIDER *interrupting:* You call it careless when the Führer is nearly killed?

SCHWEYK: A word like 'nearly' is deceptive, Mr Brett-schneider. In 1938, when they sold us out at Munich, we nearly went to war, and then when we didn't we lost nearly everything. Back in the First World War Austria nearly beat Serbia and Germany nearly beat France. You can't depend on 'nearly'.

BRETTSCHNEIDER: Go on, this is interesting. You have interesting customers, Mrs Kopecka. So well up in politics.

MRS KOPECKA: One customer's the same as another. When you're in business like me, politics don't exist. And I'd be glad, Mr Brettschneider, if you wouldn't lead my regulars on to talk politics so you can put them in prison. And as for you, Mr Schweyk, you can pay for your beer and sit your-self down and talk as much rubbish as you want. But you've talked enough, Mr Schweyk, for two glasses of Pilsener.

BRETTSCHNEIDER: I have the feeling that you wouldn't think it any great loss for the Protectorate if the Führer were lying dead at this minute.

SCHWEYK: Oh, it would be a loss, you can't say it wouldn't. A dreadful one at that. You can't replace Hitler by any old halfwit. There are a lot of people grumbling about Hitler. I'm not surprised there was an attack on him.

BRETTSCHNEIDER *hopefully:* How do you mean that exactly?

SCHWEYK *cheerfully:* Great men are always unpopular with the common herd, I read that in a leading article in 'Field

and Garden'. And for why? Because the common herd
don't understand them and find the whole thing unneces-
sary, heroism and all. The common man doesn't give a
bugger for living in a great age. He wants to go down to the
pub for a drink and have goulash for supper. What's a
statesman to do with a lot of sods like that when he's got to
get a people's name into the history books, poor bastard?
The common herd's a thorn in the flesh of any great man,
it's like Baloun with his appetite getting half a Frankfurter
for his supper, it's no good at all. I wouldn't like to hear
what the great men say about us when they all get together.

BRETTSCHNEIDER: Are you perhaps of the opinion that the
German people are not solidly behind the Führer, that they
complain?

MRS KOPECKA: Gentlemen, please change the subject, it's
all so pointless, there's a war on, don't you know?

SCHWEYK *taking a good swig of beer:* The German people are
solid behind the Führer, Mr Brettschneider, you can't say
they're not. As Marshal Goering put it, 'The Führer cannot
always be understood immediately, he is too great'. He
should know. *Confidentially:* It's amazing how many times
they've put a spoke in Hitler's wheel the moment he's got
one of his ideas, even the people up top. They say last
autumn he wanted to put up a building to stretch from
Leipzig to Dresden, a temple in memory of Germany once
it's gone under in one of his great plans he's planned down
to the last detail, and as usual they shook their heads at the
Ministry and said 'too great' because they can't understand
something incomprehensible, the sort of thing a genius
thinks up when he's got nothing better to do. Now he's
landed them in a world war just by saying he wanted the
town of Danzig, nothing more, it's the last thing he's set
his heart on. And that's the people at the top, the educated
ones, generals and directors of IG Farben, and after all they
oughtn't to mind, they don't have to pay for it. The
common man's even worse than they are. When he hears
he's to die for something great he doesn't like the taste of

it, he picks at it and pokes it around as if it was going to stick in his throat, and I ask you, isn't that going to make a Führer sick when he's made a real effort to think up something absolutely new for them, or perhaps just having a shot at conquering the world? Anyway what's left to conquer now, there are limits to that like everything else. It's all right by me.

BRETTSCHNEIDER: So you're maintaining that the Führer wants to conquer the world? That it's not just a matter of defending Germany against her Jewish enemies and the plutocracies?

SCHWEYK: Now don't you take it like that, he doesn't mean it badly, you know. Conquering the world's all in the day's work for him, like drinking beer is for you, he gets a kick out of it so anyway he'll have a go. Down with perfidious Albion. Enough said.

BRETTSCHNEIDER *standing up:* Quite enough. Come along with me to Gestapo headquarters, we'll have something to say to you there.

MRS KOPECKA: But Mr Brettschneider, Mr Schweyk has only been making quite innocent remarks, don't get him into trouble.

SCHWEYK: I'm so innocent I'm being arrested. That's two beers and a slivovitz I've had. *To Brettschneider amicably, after paying:* Pardon me going out first, but that way you'll be able to keep an eye on me and see I don't escape.

Exit Schweyk and Brettschneider.

BALOUN: And now maybe they'll shoot him.

MRS KOPECKA: You'd better have a slivovitz, Mr Prochazka. The shock went right through you, didn't it?

YOUNG PROCHAZKA: They don't dawdle over taking you away.

2

*Gestapo HQ in the Petschek Bank. Schweyk and Brettschneider are
standing in front of SS-Lieutenant Ludwig Bullinger. An SS man in
the background.*

BULLINGER: This Chalice place seems to be a nice hotbed of
subversive elements, eh?

BRETTSCHNEIDER *hurriedly:* Oh no, Lieutenant. The landlady, Mrs Kopecka, is a very respectable woman who has
nothing to do with politics; this man Schweyk is a dangerous exception among her regulars, I've had my eye on him
for quite a time. *The telephone on Bullinger's desk buzzes. He
lifts the receiver and the voice at the other end can be heard.*

VOICE ON PHONE: Mobile squad to Headquarters. Kruscha,
the banker, claims he couldn't have passed any opinions
about the attempt on the Führer's life, having been unable
to read the newspaper report as he was arrested before it
appeared.

BULLINGER: Is that the Commercial Bank fellow? Ten on
his backside. *To Schweyk:* Yes, I know your sort. First of
all I'm going to ask you a question. If you don't know the
answer, you swine, then Müller II—*pointing to the SS man—*
will take you down to the cellars for some education; d'you
understand? Here's the question: Do you shit thick or do
you shit thin?

SCHWEYK: Beg to report, sir, I shit any way you want me to.

BULLINGER: Correct answer. However, you have expressed
opinions that endanger the security of the Third Reich, you
have called the Führer's defensive war a war of conquest,
you have criticized the rationing system, and so on. What
have you got to say to all this?

SCHWEYK: It's a lot. You can have too much of a good
thing.

BULLINGER *heavily ironical:* I'm glad you're clear about that.

SCHWEYK: I'm clear about everything, stringent measures
are called for, nobody'll ever get nowhere without stringent

measures, like our sergeant used to tell us in the 91st. 'If you didn't have us to make things hot for you you'd be dropping your pants and swinging from the trees.' Just what I told myself last night when they were knocking me about.

BULLINGER: Oh, you've been knocked about, have you, now fancy that.

SCHWEYK: In the cell. One of your SS gentlemen came in and gave me one over the head with his leather belt; and when I gave a bit of a groan he turns the light on and says, 'No, that's wrong, 'tisn't this one'. And he gets so annoyed because he's wrong that he gives me another, on the back this time. But that's human nature: we go on making mistakes from the cradle to the grave.

BULLINGER: Hm. And you admit everything this says about your remarks? *Pointing to Brettschneider's report.*

SCHWEYK: If you want me to admit it, your eminence, I'll admit it, what have I to lose? But if you say, 'Schweyk, don't admit a thing', they can tear me apart and they won't get a word from me.

BULLINGER *yells:* Shut up! Take him away!

SCHWEYK *when Brettschneider has reached the door with him, raising his right arm in the Nazi salute, loudly:* Long live our Führer Adolf Hitler. Victory shall be ours!

BULLINGER *dumbfounded:* Are you a half-wit?

SCHWEYK: Beg to report, sir, yes sir. I can't help it, I've already been discharged from the army on account of half-wittedness. I have been officially certified an idiot by a medical board.

BULLINGER: Brettschneider! Didn't you see the man's a half-wit?

BRETTSCHNEIDER *injured:* Lieutenant, the observations of the man Schweyk in the Chalice resembled those of a half-wit who disguises his defeatist utterances so cleverly you can't prove anything.

BULLINGER: And you are of the opinion that what we have just heard are the observations of a man in his right mind?

BRETTSCHNEIDER: Lieutenant Bullinger, that is still my opinion. However, if for any reason you don't want him I'll take him back. I should just like to say that for us in the Criminal Investigation Department time doesn't grow on trees.

BULLINGER: Brettschneider, in my opinion you are a shit.

BRETTSCHNEIDER: Lieutenant Bullinger, I don't have to take that sort of thing from you.

BULLINGER: And I'd like you to admit it. It's not much, and it would make you feel a great deal better. Admit it, you're a shit.

BRETTSCHNEIDER: I really don't know how you can have formed such an opinion of me, Lieutenant Bullinger, in my official capacity I am conscientious down to the last detail, I . . .

VOICE ON PHONE: Mobile squad to Headquarters. The prisoner Kruscha has declared himself ready to take your brother into the bank, sir, as a partner, but continues to deny having made the remarks in question.

BULLINGER: Ten more on the backside, I need the remarks. *To Brettschneider, almost pleading:* Look, what am I asking you to do? If you admit it, it won't harm your reputation, it's a purely personal matter, you are a shit, so why not admit it? Look, I'm asking you as nicely as I can. *To Schweyk:* You try talking to him.

SCHWEYK: Beg to report, sir, that I don't want to get into an argument between you two gentlemen, but I do see what you mean, Lieutenant. But it must be a bit hard for Mr Brettschneider too, being such a good bloodhound like he is and this not really being his fault, so to speak.

BULLINGER *sadly:* So you're betraying me too, are you, you stinking hypocrite. 'And the cock crowed for the third time', like it says in the jewbible. Brettschneider, I'll wring it out of you sooner or later, but I've no time for private business just now, I've still got 97 cases to come. Throw that idiot out and once in a while try to bring me something better.

SCHWEYK *going up to him and kissing his hand:* God reward you
a thousand times, sir, and if you should ever need a dog,
you come to me, I deal in dogs.

BULLINGER: Concentration camp. *As Brettschneider is about
to take Schweyk away again:* Stop! I want to talk to this man
alone.

Exit Brettschneider, annoyed. Exit also the SS man.

VOICE ON PHONE: Mobile squad to Headquarters. The
prisoner Kruscha has admitted the remarks, but only that
he's not interested in the attempt on the Führer's life, not
that he's pleased about it, and not that the Führer's a clown,
just that he's only human after all.

BULLINGER: Five more till he's pleased about it, and till the
Führer's a bloody clown. *To Schweyk, who is smiling at him
amicably:* Do you know that in the camps we tear out your
limbs one by one if you try to take the piss out of us, you rat?

SCHWEYK: I know that. They shoot you there before you can
say Jack Robinson.

BULLINGER: So you're a dog-wallah, are you? I've seen a
pure-bred pom on the promenade that caught my fancy,
with a spot on one ear.

SCHWEYK *interrupting:* Beg to report, sir, I know that animal
professionally. There's quite a few been after that one. It
has a whiteish spot on the left ear, hasn't it? Belongs to Mr
Vojta, one of the high-ups at the Ministry. It's the apple of
his eye and only eats when it's begged to on bended knee,
and then only if it's the best cut of veal. That proves it's
racially pure. Mongrels are cleverer, but the racially pure
ones are high-class and they get stolen more often. They're
mostly so stupid they need two or three servants to tell 'em
when to shit and when to open their mouths to eat. Like
high-class people.

BULLINGER: That's enough about race, you swine. The long
and the short of it is I want that pom.

SCHWEYK: You can't have him, Vojta won't sell. What about
a police dog? The sort that can sniff out anything and track
down criminals? There's a butcher in Vršovice got one, it

pulls his cart. Now there's a dog has missed his way in life, so to speak.

BULLINGER: I told you I want that pom.

SCHWEYK: If only Mr Vojta was a Jew you could just take it away from him and that'd be that. But he's an Aryan, got a fair beard, kind of moth-eaten.

BULLINGER *interested:* Is he a real Czech?

SCHWEYK: Not what you mean, sabotaging and grumbling about Hitler, that'd be easy. Bung him into the concentration camp like me, just because I've been misunderstood. No, he's a collaborationist—they're calling him a quisling —and that makes the pom a real problem.

BULLINGER *takes a revolver out of the drawer and begins to clean it meaningly:* I can see you don't intend to get this pom for me, you saboteur.

SCHWEYK: Beg to report, sir, that I intend to get the pom. *Didactically:* There are various systems of dog-removal in use, Lieutenant. You pinch a lapdog or a terrier by cutting its lead in a crowd. You can get one of those bad-tempered dalmatians by leading a bitch on heat past it. A horsemeat sausage, nicely fried, is nearly as good. But a lot of dogs are as pampered and spoiled as the Archbishop. There was one, a smooth-haired fox terrier, pepper-and-salt he was, and I wanted him for the kennels on the other side of the Klamovka, d'you know, he wouldn't touch the sausage I gave him. Three days I followed him and then I couldn't stick it any longer, so I went straight up to the woman who used to take him for his walks and asked her what it was the dog ate made him so good-looking. That got me on the right side of her, and she said he liked chops best. So I got him a bit of fillet of veal. I thought, that's bound to be even better. And do you know, that son of a bitch wouldn't even look at it, because it was veal. He was used to pork. So I had to go and buy him a chop. I gave it him to sniff and then ran, with the dog after me. And the woman kept on shouting 'Puntik, Puntik', but it was no good, poor old Puntik. He ran after the chop as far as the corner, once he was past it I slung a chain round his neck and next day he was the other side of the Klamovka in the kennels.—But suppose people ask you where you got the dog from, when they see the spot on his ear?

BULLINGER: I don't think anybody will ask me where I got my dog from. *Rings the bell.*

SCHWEYK: Perhaps you're right there, it wouldn't do them much good, would it?

BULLINGER: And I think you've put one over on me about being certified as an idiot; but I'm ready to turn a blind eye to that, for one thing because Brettschneider's a shit and for another because you're going to get me that dog for my wife, you crook.

SCHWEYK: Sir, permission to admit that I really was certified, though I was having a bit of a joke as well. As the landlord of a pub in Budweis said, 'I'm an epileptic but I've got cancer as well', when he wanted to keep it dark that he'd gone bankrupt. It's like the old Czech proverb says, sweaty feet seldom come singly.

VOICE ON PHONE: Mobile squad number 4 to Headquarters. The prisoner Moudra Greissler denies having overstepped the regulations relating to shops not opening before 9 a.m. on the grounds that she didn't in fact open her shop till 10 a.m.

BULLINGER: Crafty bitch. Couple of months inside for understepping the regulations. *To the SS man who has just come in, indicating Schweyk:* Free till further notice.

SCHWEYK: Before I do go, could I put in a word for a gentleman that's waiting outside among the prisoners, so he doesn't have to sit with the others, you see it isn't very nice for him, it looks a bit suspicious, him sitting on the same bench with us political prisoners. He's only here for attempted murder of a farmer from Holice.

BULLINGER *roars:* Clear out!

SCHWEYK: Very good, sir. I'll bring the pom as soon as I've got it. A very good morning!
Exit with the SS man.

INTERLUDE IN THE LOWER REGIONS

Schweyk and SS man Müller II in conversation on their way from SS headquarters to the Chalice.

SCHWEYK: If I tell Mrs Kopecka, she might do it for you. I'm glad to hear you confirm that the Führer doesn't go for the girls, so that he can reserve his strength for higher matters of State, and that he don't ever drink alcohol. He's done what he has done stone-cold sober, you might say; it's not everyone who'd do the same. And it's lucky too that he doesn't eat anything except a few vegetables and a bit of pastry, because there's not much going, what with the war and all that, and it makes one mouth less to feed. I knew a farmer up in Moravia who'd got stomach trouble and had no appetite, and his farmhands got so scraggy that the whole village began to talk, and the farmer just went around saying 'In my house the servants eat what I eat'. Drinking's a vice, I admit, like old Budova the saddler, who meant to swindle his brother and then while he was under the influence signed over his own inheritance to the brother instead of the other way round. There are two sides to everything, and he wouldn't have to give up the girls if it were left to me, I don't ask that of anybody.

3

In the Chalice Baloun is waiting for his meal. Two other customers are playing draughts, a fat female shopkeeper is enjoying a small slivovitz, and Mrs Kopecka is knitting.

BALOUN: It's ten past twelve now, and no Prochazka. As I expected.

MRS KOPECKA: Give him a bit of time. The quickest aren't always the best. You need the right mixture of fast and slow. Do you know the 'Song of the Gentle Breeze'? *She sings:*

Come here, my dearest, and make haste
No one dearer could I pick
But once your arm is round my waist
Don't try to be too quick.
  Learn from the plums in the autumn
  All golden on the trees.
  They fear the whirlwind's terrible strength
  And long for the gentle breeze.
  You can scarcely feel that gentle breeze
  It's like a whispering lullaby
  Which makes the plums drop off the trees
  Till on the ground they lie.

Oh, reaper, don't cut all the grass
But leave *one* blade to grow.
Don't drain the brimming wine-glass
Don't kiss me as you go.
  Learn from the plums in the autumn
  All golden on the trees.
  They fear the whirlwind's terrible strength
  And long for the gentle breeze.
  You can scarcely feel that gentle breeze
  It's like a whispering lullaby
  Which makes the plums drop off the trees
  Till on the ground they lie.

BALOUN *restless, going over to the draughts players:* You're in a good position. Would you gentlemen be interested in postcards? I work at a photographer's, and we're putting out a series of special postcards on the quiet: it's called 'German towns'.

FIRST CUSTOMER: I'm not interested in German towns.

BALOUN: You'll like our series then. *He shows them postcards furtively, as if they were pornographic pictures.* That's Cologne.

FIRST CUSTOMER: That looks dreadful. I'll have that one. Nothing but craters.

BALOUN: Fifty Hellers. But be careful showing it around. We've already had police patrols picking up people who were showing it to one another, because they thought it was something filthy, the sort of thing they like to confiscate.

FIRST CUSTOMER: That's a good caption: 'Hitler is one of the greatest architects of all time'. And a picture of Bremen in a heap of rubble.

BALOUN: I sold two dozen to a German NCO. He grinned when he looked at them, and I liked that. I told him I'd meet him in the park by Havliček's statue, and I kept my knife open in my pocket in case he was a twister. But he was straight.

FAT WOMAN: He who lives by the sword shall perish by the sword.

MRS KOPECKA: Careful!

Enter Schweyk with SS man Müller II, a beanpole of a man.

SCHWEYK: Morning all. This gentleman with me isn't on duty. Let us have a glass of beer, Mrs Kopecka.

BALOUN: I didn't think we'd be seeing you again for a good few years. Ah well, we all make mistakes. Mr Brettschneider's usually so thorough. Last week, when you weren't here, he took the upholsterer in Cross Lane away and he hasn't come back since.

SCHWEYK: Must have been some awkward fellow who didn't crawl to them. Mr Brettschneider will think twice before he misunderstands me again. I've got protection.

FAT WOMAN: Are you the one they took away here yesterday?

SCHWEYK *proudly:* The very man. In times like these you've got to crawl. It's a matter of practice. I licked his hand. In the old days they used to put salt on prisoners' faces. Then they tied them up and set great wolfhounds on to them, and the dogs'ld lick away their whole faces, I believe. Nowadays people aren't so cruel, except when they lose their tempers. Oh, but I was forgetting: this gentleman—*indicating the SS man*—wants to know what good things the future has in store for him, Mrs Kopecka, and two beers. I've told him you've got second sight and I think it's creepy and he should have nothing to do with it.

MRS KOPECKA: You know I don't like doing it, Mr Schweyk.

SS MAN: Why don't you like to, young lady?

MRS KOPECKA: A gift like that is a responsibility. How are you to tell which way a person is going to take it, or if he's got strength enough to face up to it? Because a look into the future sometimes gets a person really on the raw, and then he blames it on me, like Czaka the brewer, I had to tell him that pretty young wife of his was going to deceive him, and right off he went and broke a valuable mirror I had on the wall there.

SCHWEYK: But she led him a dance all right. And Blaukopf the schoolmaster, we told his fortune too, same thing it was. And it always happens, when she predicts something like that. I think it's quite remarkable. The way you told Councillor Czerlek that his wife, remember, Mrs Kopecka? And she did.

SS MAN: But you've a rare gift there, you know, and you shouldn't let a thing like that go to waste.

SCHWEYK: I've told her before now she ought to make the same prediction to the entire Council, I wouldn't be surprised if it came true.

MRS KOPECKA: Don't joke about such things, Mr Schweyk. They exist, and that's all we know about them because they're supernatural.

SCHWEYK: And do you remember how you told Bulova the engineer, here, right to his face, that he'd be cut to pieces in a railway accident? His wife's already got married again. Women can stand prediction better, they've more strength of character, I'm told. Mrs Laslaček in Huss Street had such strength of character that her husband said in public: 'Anything rather than live with that woman', and went off as a voluntary worker to Germany. But the SS can stand quite a lot too, I'm told, they have to what with the concentration camps and that third-degree stuff, you've got to have nerves of steel for that sort of thing, haven't you? *SS man nods.* So you don't have to worry about telling the gentleman's fortune, Mrs Kopecka.

MRS KOPECKA: If he'll promise to treat it as a harmless game and not take it seriously, I might just have a look at his hand.

SS MAN *suddenly hesitant:* I don't want to force you, you say you don't like doing it.

MRS KOPECKA *bringing him his beer:* Quite right. Better forget it and drink your beer.

FAT WOMAN *aside to draughts player:* Cotton's a help if you suffer from cold feet.

SCHWEYK *sits down beside Baloun:* I've some business to discuss with you, I'm going to collaborate with the Germans about a dog, and I need you.

BALOUN: I'm not in the mood.

SCHWEYK: There'll be something in it for you. If you had the cash you could take your appetite along to the black market and get something for it.

BALOUN: Young Prochazka isn't coming. Nothing but mashed potatoes again, one more disappointment like this and I'll never get over it.

SCHWEYK: Perhaps we might form a little club, six or seven chaps who'd be ready to put their two ounces of meat together, and then you'd get your meal.

BALOUN: Where would we find them, though?

SCHWEYK: That's true, it probably wouldn't work. They'd say they weren't going to give up their rations for a blot on the landscape like you, without the strength of mind to be a real Czech.

BALOUN *glumly:* Yes, you're right, they'd tell me to bugger off.

SCHWEYK: Can't you pull yourself together and think of the honour of your country whenever you feel this temptation and all you can see is a leg of veal or a nice fried pork fillet with a bit of red cabbage or gherkins maybe? *Baloun groans.* Just think of the disgrace if you gave way.

BALOUN: I'll have to try, I suppose. *Pause.* I'd sooner have red cabbage than gherkins, if it's all the same to you.

Young Prochazka enters with a briefcase.

SCHWEYK: There he is. You were looking too much on the black side, Baloun. Good morning, Mr Prochazka, how's business?

BALOUN: Good morning, Mr Prochazka, I'm glad you're here.

MRS KOPECKA *glancing at the SS man:* Will you join these gentlemen, I've something to do first. *To the SS man:* I think your hand might interest me after all, could I just have a look? *She takes hold of it.* I thought so; you have an extraordinarily interesting hand. I mean a hand that's almost irresistible for us astrologers and palmists, as interesting as that. How many other gentlemen are there in your unit?

SS MAN *with difficulty, as if having a tooth extracted:* In the detachment? Twenty. Why?

MRS KOPECKA: I thought so. It's in your hand. There are twenty gentlemen associated with you in life and death.

SS MAN: Can you really see that in my hand?

SCHWEYK *who has joined them, gaily:* You'll be surprised what else she can see there. It's just that she's careful, she won't say anything that's not absolutely certain.

MRS KOPECKA: Your hand has a lot of electricity in it, you're lucky in love, that's clear from the well-formed Mount of Venus. Women throw themselves at you, so to speak, but then they are often pleasantly surprised and wouldn't have missed the experience for worlds. You're a serious personality, and you can be tough. Your success line is fantastic.

SS MAN: What does that mean?

MRS KOPECKA: It's nothing to do with money, it's much more than that. Do you see that H, the three lines there? That means heroism, something heroic you're going to do, and very soon at that.

SS MAN: Where? Can you see where?

MRS KOPECKA: Not here. Not in your own country either. Quite a way off. There's something peculiar here that I can't quite understand. There's a secret hanging over this, so to speak, as if only you yourself and those with you at the time are going to know about it, nobody apart from that, never afterwards either.

SS MAN: How can that be?

MRS KOPECKA *sighing:* I don't know, perhaps it's on the battlefield, some forward position or something like that. *As if confused:* But that's enough, isn't it? I've got to get on with my work, and it is just a game, you promised me.

SS MAN: But you can't stop now. I want to know more about this secret, Mrs Kopecka.

SCHWEYK: I think so too, you ought not to keep the man guessing. *Mrs Kopecka winks at him in such a way that the SS man can see.* But perhaps you have said enough, because, well, there's a lot we're better off not knowing. Varczek the schoolmaster once looked in the encyclopaedia to see what skizziphonia meant, and afterwards they had to take him off to the Ilmenau asylum.

SS MAN: There was something more you saw in my hand.

MRS KOPECKA: No, no, that was all. Leave me alone.

SS MAN: You don't want to tell me. I saw you winking at this fellow to get him to stop, because you didn't want to speak, but I'm not having that sort of thing.

SCHWEYK: That's right, Mrs Kopecka, the SS won't have that sort of thing. I had to speak right away at Gestapo headquarters, like it or not, and straight off I admitted I wished the Führer a long life.

MRS KOPECKA: Nobody can force me to tell a customer things he won't want to hear so that he never comes back here.

SS MAN: There you are, you know something and you're not saying. You've given yourself away.

MRS KOPECKA: The second H isn't at all clear anyway: not one in a hundred would notice it.

SS MAN: What second H is that?

SCHWEYK: Get me another pint, Mrs Kopecka, it's so exciting I'm getting a thirst.

MRS KOPECKA: It's always the same, you just get yourself in trouble if you give in and do your best to read a hand. *Brings Schweyk's beer.* I didn't expect the second H, but if it's there, what can I do about it? If I tell you you'll be depressed, and it isn't as if there's anything you can do.

SS MAN: But what is it?

SCHWEYK *genially:* It must be something serious if I know Mrs Kopecka, I've never seen her like this before, and she's seen lots of things in people's hands. Can you really bear it, do you feel up to it?

SS MAN *hoarsely:* What is it?

MRS KOPECKA: And then if I tell you that the second H means a hero's death, at any rate usually, and then it depresses you? There you are, you see, it's taken you badly. I knew it. Three beers, that makes two crowns.

SS MAN *pays, shattered:* It's all a load of nonsense. Reading your hand. It can't be done.

SCHWEYK: You're quite right, look on the bright side.

SS MAN *going:* Heil Hitler.

MRS KOPECKA *calling after him:* Promise me at least you won't tell the others.

SS MAN *stops:* What others?

SCHWEYK: Your detachment. You know, the twenty of them.

SS MAN: What's it got to do with them?

MRS KOPECKA: It's just that they're associated with you in life and death. I don't want them to worry unnecessarily. *Exit SS man, cursing.*

MRS KOPECKA: Do come again.

FAT WOMAN *laughing:* Lovely. You're pure gold, Mrs Kopecka.

SCHWEYK: That's that detachment dealt with. Unpack your briefcase, Mr Prochazka. Baloun won't be able to stand it much longer.

MRS KOPECKA: Yes, bring it out, Rudolf. It's good of you to have brought it.

YOUNG PROCHAZKA *feebly:* I haven't got it. Seeing them take Mr Schweyk away gave me such a shock I kept seeing it all night long, good morning Mr Schweyk, so you're back, I didn't dare to risk it, I'm afraid. I feel dreadful, Mrs Kopecka, letting you down in front of the customers, but it's stronger than I am. *Desperately:* Please say something, anything's better than this silence.

BALOUN: Nothing.

MRS KOPECKA: Well, so you haven't got it. But before, when you came in, when I gave you a sign that I'd have to get rid of the SS man first, you nodded to me as if you'd got it.

YOUNG PROCHAZKA: I didn't dare ...

MRS KOPECKA: You needn't say any more. I've got your mark. You've failed the test as a man and as a Czech. Get out, you coward, and never darken my doors again.

YOUNG PROCHAZKA: It's all I deserve. *Slinks away.*

SCHWEYK *after a pause:* Talking of palmistry, Krisch the barber at Mnišek—you know Mnišek?—was telling people's fortunes from their hands at the parish fair, and got himself drunk on the proceeds, and a young farmer took him home with him so he could tell his fortune when he'd sobered up, and before he fell asleep the barber asked this young fellow 'What are you called? Get my notebook out of my inside pocket, will you? So you're called Kunert. Right, come back in a quarter of an hour and I'll leave you a bit of paper with the name of your future wife on it'. And with that old Krisch began to snore. But then he woke up again and scribbled something in his notebook. He tore it out and threw it on the floor and put his finger to his lips and said 'Not now, in a quarter of an hour. It'll be best if you look for the bit of paper blindfold'. And all there was on the paper was 'The name of your future wife will be Mrs Kunert'.

BALOUN: He's a criminal, that Prochazka.

MRS KOPECKA *angrily:* Don't talk nonsense. The criminals are the Nazis, threatening and torturing people for so long that they go against their real nature. *Looking through the window:* This one coming now, he's a criminal, not Rudolf Prochazka; he's just weak.

FAT WOMAN: I tell you, we're guilty as well. We might do a bit more than drink slivovitz and make jokes.

SCHWEYK: Don't ask too much of yourself. It's something to be still alive nowadays. And you're kept so busy keeping alive that there's no time for anything else.

Enter Brettschneider and the SS man of the previous day.

SCHWEYK *gaily:* A very good morning to you, Mr Brettschneider. Will you have a beer with me? I'm working for the SS now, so it can't do me any harm.

BALOUN *viciously:* Out!

BRETTSCHNEIDER: How exactly do you mean that?

SCHWEYK: We've been talking of food, and Mr Baloun has just remembered the chorus of a popular song we've been trying to call to mind. It's a song they usually sing at fairs, about the proper way to deal with radishes, around Mnišek they have those big black radishes, you'll have heard about them, they're famous. I'd be glad if you'd sing that song for Mr Brettschneider, Baloun, it would cheer him up. He has a fine voice, he even sings in the church choir.

BALOUN *scowling:* I'll sing it. The subject is radishes.

Baloun sings the 'Song of the Black Radish'. All through the song Brettschneider, with everyone looking at him, is undecided whether to intervene or not. Each time he sits down again.

It's always best to pick a nice fat black one
And gaily tell him, 'Oy, mate, you get out'.
But wear your gloves when you attack one
Bang on the snout.
That snout's so dirty 'cause the bugger lives in dung.
Filthy lout. Should be slung
Out.

You won't be asked to pay inflated prices
You get the sod dirt cheap all over town.

And once you've got him shredded into slices
Salt him down.
  Salt in his wounds! He's asked for everything he gets.
  Salt him down! Till he sweats.
  Salt him down!

INTERLUDE IN THE HIGHER REGIONS

*Hitler and Marshal Goering in front of a model tank. Both are
larger than life. Martial music.*

HITLER
  My good old Goering, now three hard-fought years have
    passed
  And it looks as if my war's won at last
  Though it's hard to keep it from spreading to other areas
  Unless I can have more tanks, guns and aircraft carriers.
  That means people have got to stop sitting around and
    flopping
  And start sweating blood for my war instead until they're
    dropping.
  So answer me if you can:
  What of the European *Little Man*?
  D'you think he'll want to work for my war?
GOERING
  Mein Führer, I'd say that is something of which we're quite
    sure:
  The Little Man in Europe will sweat out his guts no less
    cheerfully
  Than the Little Man in Germany.
  That's a job for my Labour Front.
HITLER
  Splendid, so you've got a special outfit. That's an excellent
    stunt.

4

*A bench in the gardens by the Moldau. Evening. A couple enter,
stand looking upstage towards the river with their arms round each
other, saunter on. Enter Schweyk and Baloun. They look back.*

SCHWEYK: Old Vojta treats his servant girls pretty badly;
she's the third he's had since Candlemas, and already wanting to leave, I'm told, because their neighbours are on at her
for working for a quisling. So it doesn't matter to her if she
comes home without the dog, so long as it's not her fault.
You sit down there first, she mightn't sit down if nobody
else is sitting there.

BALOUN: Shouldn't I be holding the sausage?

SCHWEYK: So you can eat it yourself? Just sit down.

*Baloun sits down on the bench. Two servant girls enter, Anna and
Kati, the former with a pomeranian on a lead.*

SCHWEYK: Excuse me, miss, can you tell me how I get to
Palacky Street?

KATI *distrustful:* It's just across Havlíček Square. Come on,
Anna.

SCHWEYK: Excuse me, but can you tell me where the square
is? I'm a stranger here.

ANNA: I'm a stranger too. Go on, Kati, tell the gentleman.

SCHWEYK: Well now, isn't it funny that you should be a
stranger too. I'd never have known you weren't a Prague
girl, and with such a nice little dog. Where do you come
from?

ANNA: I'm from Protivin.

SCHWEYK: Then we're almost neighbours, I'm from Budweis.

KATI *trying to draw her away:* Do come on, Anna.

ANNA: Coming. Then you must know Pejchara, the butcher
with the shop on the ring road in Budweis.

SCHWEYK: Do I know him? He's my brother. He's very well
liked there, you know, a nice chap and very obliging, and
always the best meat and good measure.

ANNA: Yes.

Pause. Kati waits ironically.

SCHWEYK: What a coincidence we should meet as far away as this. Have you a few minutes to spare? We must tell each other the news from Budweis—there's a bench over there with a nice view—that's the Moldau.

KATI: Really? *With pointed irony:* I'd never have known.

ANNA: There's somebody sitting there already.

SCHWEYK: A gentleman enjoying the view. You should keep an eye on that dog of yours.

ANNA: Why?

SCHWEYK: Don't say I told you, but the Germans are keen on dogs, astonishingly keen, specially the SS, a dog like that's gone quick as a wink, they ship 'em back home, me for instance, only the other day I met an SS lieutenant called Bullinger who was looking for a pom for his wife back in Cologne.

KATI: So you knock around with SS lieutenants and people like that, do you? Come on, Anna, that really is enough.

SCHWEYK: I spoke to him while I was in custody for expressing opinions that endangered the security of the Third Reich.

KATI: Is that true? Then I take back what I said. We've got a few minutes to spare, Anna.

She leads the way to the bench. The three of them sit down next to Baloun.

KATI: What opinions?

SCHWEYK *indicates that he cannot talk about it because of the stranger, and adopts an especially innocent tone:* How do you like it in Prague?

ANNA: All right, but you can't trust the men here.

SCHWEYK: That's only too true, I'm glad you realize it. Country people are a decenter lot, wouldn't you say? *To Baloun:* Nice view here, sir, don't you think?

BALOUN: Not bad.

SCHWEYK: Sort of view would appeal to a photographer.

BALOUN: As a background.

SCHWEYK: A photographer could make something really nice out of it.

BALOUN: I am a photographer. We've got the Moldau painted on a screen in the studio where I work, only a bit tarted up. We use it for the Germans, mostly SS, who want a picture of themselves in front of it to send home when they've been posted and won't be coming back. It isn't the Moldau, though, just any old river.

The girls laugh approvingly.

SCHWEYK: That's very interesting. Couldn't you maybe take a snap of the young ladies—needn't be a full-length shot, just a bust—beg pardon, that's the technical term.

BALOUN: I could indeed.

ANNA: That would be nice. But not in front of that Moldau of yours, eh?

Plenty of laughter greets this, then a pause.

SCHWEYK: D'you know this one? A Czech standing on the Charles Bridge hears a German in the Moldau shouting for help. So he leans over the parapet and yells 'Shut up down there, you ought to have learnt swimming instead of German'.

The girls laugh.

SCHWEYK: Yes, that's the Moldau. There's a lot of immorality goes on in the park now it's wartime, I can tell you.

KATI: There was in peacetime.

BALOUN: And at Whitsun.

SCHWEYK: Out of doors they keep at it till All Saints' Day.

KATI: And nothing goes on indoors?

BALOUN: Plenty there too.

ANNA: And at the pictures.

They all laugh a lot again.

SCHWEYK: Yes, the Moldau. D'you know the old song 'Henry slept beside his newly-wedded'? They sing it a lot in Moravia.

ANNA: Doesn't it go on 'Heiress to a castle on the Rhine'?

SCHWEYK: Yes, that's the one. *To Baloun:* Have you got

something in your eye? Don't rub it. Could you perhaps see to it, Miss, the corner of a handkerchief's the best.

ANNA *to Schweyk:* Would you hold the dog? You've got to be careful in Prague. There's a lot of soot blows around.

SCHWEYK *ties the dog loosely to the lamppost near the bench:* Excuse me, but I really must get down to Palacky Street. Business you know. I should like to have heard you sing the song, but I haven't the time, I'm afraid. Good-bye. *Exit.*

KATI *as Anna fishes around in Baloun's eye with a handkerchief:* He's in a hurry.

ANNA: I can't find anything.

BALOUN: It's better, I think. What's this song you were talking about?

ANNA: Shall we sing it for you? We really must go then, though. Quiet, Lux. I'd be glad to see the back of both you and your master. *To Baloun:* He's too well in with the Germans for me. Right, I'll begin.

The two girls sing 'Henry slept beside his newly-wedded'* with considerable feeling. Meanwhile from behind a bush Schweyk attracts the dog with a tiny sausage, and makes off with it.

BALOUN *after the song:* You sang that beautifully.

KATI: And now we've really got to go. Mother of God, where's the dog?

ANNA: Heavens above, now the dog's gone. And he never runs away. What will Mr Vojta say?

BALOUN: He'll ring up his friends the Germans, that's all. Don't get upset, it's not your fault, that gentleman can't have tied him tight enough. I thought I caught a glimpse of something moving away while you were singing.

KATI: Quick, we'll go to the police and see if it's been found.

BALOUN: Why don't you come to the Chalice one Saturday night. It's number 7, Huss Street.

They nod to Baloun and go out quickly. Baloun returns to his contemplation of the view. The previous couple come back, but with their arms no longer round each other. Then Schweyk arrives with the pomeranian on a lead.

* The text of this song is on p. 139.

SCHWEYK: It's a real quisling's dog, bites when you're not looking. Gave me a terrible time on the way. When I was crossing the railway he lay down on the lines and wouldn't move. Perhaps he wanted to commit suicide, the silly sod. Let's get a move on.

BALOUN: Did he go for that horse sausage? I thought he was only supposed to eat veal.

SCHWEYK: War's no picnic, not even for them with pedigrees. But Bullinger's not getting this one till I see the colour of his money, or else he'll swindle me. Us collaborators have to be paid.

A tall, sinister man has appeared upstage and has been watching the two of them. He now approaches.

MAN: Good evening, gentlemen. Taking a stroll?

SCHWEYK: Yes, and what's it got to do with you?

MAN: Perhaps you'd be kind enough to show me your identification papers. *He displays an official badge.*

SCHWEYK: I haven't got my papers with me, have you?

BALOUN *shakes his head:* We've not done anything.

MAN: I didn't stop you because you'd done something, but because you seemed to me to be doing nothing. I'm from the Department of Voluntary War Work.

SCHWEYK: Are you one of those gentlemen who have to hang around outside cinemas and in pubs to dig up people for the factories?

MAN: What's your job?

SCHWEYK: I run a dog business.

MAN: Have you got a certificate to say you're employed on essential war work?

SCHWEYK: No, your honour, I haven't. But it is essential war work; even in wartime a chap wants a dog, so that he can have a friend at his side when the bad times come, eh, pom? People keep a lot calmer when they're being bombed and shelled if they've got a dog looking up at them like he was saying 'Is that really necessary?' And this gentleman is a photographer, and that's even more essential if anything, because he takes photos of soldiers so that the folks back home can at least have pictures of their boys, and that's better than nothing, you must admit.

MAN: I think I'd better take you along to headquarters, and I advise you to cut out all this nonsense when you get there,

BALOUN: But we pinched the dog under higher orders, can't you explain to him?

SCHWEYK: There's nothing to explain. This fellow's under higher orders too.

They leave with him.

SCHWEYK: So your job is pinching men, is it?

5

Lunch time in the Prague goods yards. On the rails sit Schweyk and Baloun, now shunters in the service of Hitler, guarded by a German soldier armed to the teeth.

BALOUN: I'd like to know what's happened to Mrs Kopecka with our dinner. I hope she's not got into trouble.

SERVICE CORPS LIEUTENANT *passing, to Soldier:* Guard! If anyone asks which is the waggon for Bavaria, remember it's that one there, number 4268.

SOLDIER *at attention:* Yessir.

SCHWEYK: It's all organization with the Germans. They've got things better organized than anyone ever before. Hitler presses a button and bang goes—China, let's say. They've got the Pope in Rome on their list, with all he's said about 'em, he's had it. And even lower down the scale, take an SS commander, he's only got to press the button and there's the urn with your ashes being handed to your widow. We can thank our stars we're here with a well-armed guard to stop us sabotaging something and getting shot.

Mrs Kopecka enters with enamel dishes. The soldier studies her pass absently.

BALOUN: What is it?

MRS KOPECKA: Carrot cutlet and potato sausages. *As the two of them eat the food with their plates on their knees, softly:* That dog must go. It's become a political matter now. Don't gobble, Mr Baloun, you'll get ulcers.

BALOUN: Not from potatoes I shan't, from a nice fat chicken maybe.

MRS KOPECKA: It said in the paper the disappearance of Councillor Vojta's dog was an act of vengeance by a section of the population against a pro-German official. Now they're looking for it so they can smoke out the nest of subversive elements. It must be got out of the Chalice, and today.

SCHWEYK: It isn't very convenient at the moment. Only yesterday I sent Lieutenant Bullinger an express letter saying I wanted 200 crowns for the dog and I wouldn't let him have it till I got the money.

MRS KOPECKA: Mr Schweyk, you're taking your life in your hands writing letters like that.

SCHWEYK: I don't think so, Mrs Kopecka. Bullinger's a swine, but he'll find it quite natural that business is business, otherwise nothing's sacred, and he needs the dog for his wife in Cologne, I'm told. A collaborationist doesn't work for nothing, just the opposite, he even gets paid more these days because his own people despise him, I have to be compensated for that, why else do it?

MRS KOPECKA: But you can't do business while you're stuck here.

SCHWEYK *amiably:* I'm not wasting my time here. I've already cost them one waggonload of soap. It isn't difficult. In Austria once, when they banned strikes, the railwaymen stopped traffic for eight hours just by carrying out all the safety regulations to the letter.

MRS KOPECKA *energetically:* All the same, that dog must be got out of the Chalice, Mr Schweyk. I have a certain amount of protection from Mr Brettschneider, who's still hoping to start something with me, but that won't go far. *Schweyk is only half listening to her, as two German soldiers have been taking a great steaming cooking-pot past and serving goulash into the guard's aluminium plate. Baloun, who has long since finished eating, has stood up, and as if in a trance is following the trail of the food, sniffing.*

SCHWEYK: I'll come and get him. Just look at that!

GERMAN SOLDIER *shouting sharply at Baloun:* Halt!

MRS KOPECKA *to Baloun, as he comes back discontented and upset:* Do pull yourself together, Mr Baloun.

SCHWEYK: In Budweis there was a doctor who had diabetes so bad that all he was allowed to eat was a tiny bit of rice pudding, and him a great barrel of a man. He couldn't keep it up and went on eating the leftovers in the pantry on the quiet. He knew just what he was doing and after a bit he decided it was all too silly, so he told his housekeeper to cook him a seven-course meal, pudding and all, and she cried so much she could hardly dish it up, and he put a funeral march on the gramophone to go with it and that was the end of him. It'll be just the same with you, Baloun, you'll finish up under a Russian tank.

BALOUN *still shivering from top to toe:* They're handing out goulash.

MRS KOPECKA: I've got to go. *She picks up the dishes and leaves.*

BALOUN: I only want to have a look. *To the soldier, who is eating:* Are the helpings always as big as that in the army, soldier? That's a nice big one you've got. But maybe it's only when you're on guard, so you can keep wide awake, or else we might clear off, eh? Could I just have a sniff maybe?

The soldier sits eating, but between bites he moves his lips.

SCHWEYK: Don't bother him with questions. Can't you see he's got to learn the number by heart, or he'll be sending the wrong waggon off to Bavaria, you idiot? *To the soldier:* You're right to make sure you know it, anything can happen. They've stopped putting the destinations on the waggons now because saboteurs used to rub them off and write the wrong address on. What was that number: 4268, wasn't it? Look, you don't need to keep saying it under your breath for half an hour, let me tell you what to do, I got this tip from an official in the department where they issue licences to traders, he was explaining it to a pedlar who couldn't remember his number. I'll show you how it works for yours and you'll see how easy it is. 4268. The first figure is a 4, the second a 2. So the first thing to remember is 42. That's twice two, or starting the other way round, it's 4 divided by 2, and there you've got your 4 and your 2 next to each other again. Don't get alarmed now; what's twice 4? 8, isn't it? Right, fix in your memory that the 8 in 4268 is the last in the series, and the only other thing you need remember is that the first figure is a 4, the second a 2, the fourth an 8, and then you just need some good way of remembering the 6 that comes before the 8. It's dead easy. The first figure is a 4, the second a 2, 4 and 2 is 6. So you're quite clear that the second number from the end is a 6, and now, as the man at the licensing office would have said, the order of the figures is permanently fixed in our memory. You can get the same result even easier. He explained this method to the pedlar too. I'll do it again for you with your number.

The soldier has been listening wide-eyed. His lips have stopped moving.

SCHWEYK: 8 less 2 is 6. So there's your 6. 6 less 2 is 4, so there's your 4. 8 and the 2 in between gives you 4–2–6–8. It's easy enough to do it another way again, using multiplication and division. This is how you get the answer then: he said you must remember that twice 42 is 84. There are 12 months in a year. So you take 12 from 84, that leaves us with 72; take off another 12 months, that's 60. So that's our 6 fixed, and we cancel the nought. Now we've got 42–6–84. Since we've cancelled the nought we also cancel the 4 at the end, and there we've got our number complete again. You can do it with division too, like this. What was our number, by the way?

VOICE OFF: Guard, what's the number of the waggon for Bavaria?

SOLDIER: What is it?

SCHWEYK: Right, just a moment, I'll work it out by the system with the months. There are 12 of them, aren't there —agreed?

SOLDIER *desperately:* Tell me the number.

VOICE: Guard! Are you asleep?

SOLDIER *shouts:* I've forgotten it. For-got-ten! *To Schweyk:* To hell with you!

VOICE *roughly:* It's got to go with the 12.50 to Passau.

SECOND VOICE *further off:* Let's take this one then, I think that's it.

BALOUN *satisfied, indicating the soldier, who is looking upstage appalled:* He wouldn't let me sniff his goulash.

SCHWEYK: For all I know a waggonload of machine-guns is on its way to Bavaria now. *Philosophically:* But by that time perhaps what they'll need most in Stalingrad will be combine-harvesters and it'll be Bavaria's turn to want machine-guns. Who can tell?

6

Saturday night at the Chalice. Among the customers Baloun, Anna, Kati, Young Prochazka and two SS men on their own. Dancing to the music of a player piano.

KATI *to Baloun:* I told Mr Brettschneider at the inquiry that I'd already heard the SS were after the dog. I didn't mention your name, only your friend Mr Schweyk's. And I didn't say anything about Mr Schweyk pretending he didn't know you so he could get into conversation with us. Was that all right?

BALOUN: Anything's all right as far as I am concerned. I won't be with you much longer. They'll not half be surprised to see me.

ANNA: Don't be so gloomy, Mr Baloun, it doesn't help. And

that SS man over there will ask me to dance again if I go on sitting around like this. You ask me.

Baloun is about to get up when Mrs Kopecka comes downstage and claps her hands.

MRS KOPECKA: Ladies and gentlemen, it's coming up to half past eight, time for the Beseda—*partly to the SS men*—our traditional dance we dance among ourselves, it mayn't please everyone but we like it. The music's on the house. *Mrs Kopecka puts a coin in the piano and the company dance the Beseda, stamping very loudly. Baloun and Anna join in. The aim of the dance is to get rid of the SS men, and so their table is barged into, etc.*

BALOUN *sings:*

When the midnight churchbells ring
Feel your oats and have a fling.
Yupp-i-diddle, yupp-i-day
Girls come out to play.

THE OTHERS *join in:*

Let you pinch their rosy cheeks
Most of them have four cheeks each
Yupp-i-diddle, yupp-i-day
Girls come out to play.

The SS men stand up swearing, and push their way out. After the dance Mrs Kopecka comes in again from the back room and goes on rinsing her glasses. Kati brings the first customer of scene 3 over to her table.

FIRST CUSTOMER: Folk dancing's a new idea at the Chalice. Very popular it is; the regulars know Mrs Kopecka listens to Radio Moscow while it's going on.

BALOUN: I shan't be dancing with you much longer. Where I'm going they don't dance the Beseda.

ANNA: I'm told we were very rash to go into the Moldau gardens. It's dangerous because of the German deserters who set on you.

FIRST CUSTOMER: They only go for men. They're after civilian clothes. There's German uniforms being found every morning now in Stromovka Park.

KATI: And anybody loses his suit that way doesn't find it so easy to get a new one. They say the Clothes Rationing Bureau have stopped clothes and hats being made out of paper now. Because of the paper shortage.

FIRST CUSTOMER: Clothes Rationing Bureau! The Germans just love bureaus, they spring up like mushrooms all over the place. It's a matter of making jobs for themselves so they aren't called up. They'd rather torment us Czechs with milk rationing and food rationing and paper rationing and all the rest. Scrimshankers.

BALOUN: They'll finish me off. I can see only one future for me.

ANNA: What on earth are you talking about?

BALOUN: You'll find out soon enough, Anna. I suppose you know that song 'Myriad doors and gateways' about the painter who died young. Would you sing it for me, it's my case exactly.

ANNA *sings:*

Myriad doors and gateways he could paint you straight-ways

Loved his decorating, kept no lady waiting.

You won't see him around, he's six feet underground.

—You mean that one?

BALOUN: That's it.

ANNA: But heavens, you're not going to make away with yourself, Mr Baloun?

BALOUN: What I'm going to do to myself will fill you with horror, Anna. I'm not taking my life but something much worse.

Enter Schweyk with a parcel under his arm.

SCHWEYK *to Baloun:* Here I am with your goulash meat. You needn't thank me, because I'm having that camp bed in your kitchen in exchange.

BALOUN: Show me, is it beef?

SCHWEYK *energetically:* Take your paws off it. It's not to be unpacked here. Good evening, ladies, are you here too?

ANNA: Good evening. We know all about it.

SCHWEYK *pulling Baloun into a corner:* What have you been letting out now?

BALOUN: Only that we know each other and it was a trick pretending we didn't. I didn't know anything to let out. You're welcome to my camp bed. You've saved a friend from the edge of the precipice, just let me sniff it through the paper. Mrs Mahler from across the road offered me 20 crowns for it, but I'm not interested. Where did you get this?

SCHWEYK: On the black market, from a midwife who got it from the country. About 1930 she delivered a farmer's child with a little bone in its mouth, and she burst into tears and said 'That means we'll all go hungry', that's what she predicted long before the Germans were here, and every year the farmer's wife sends her a food parcel so she won't go hungry, but this year the midwife needs the money to pay her taxes.

BALOUN: Let's hope Mrs Kopecka has some real paprika.

MRS KOPECKA *who has joined them:* Go back to your table, in half an hour I'll call you into the kitchen. And in the meantime act as if nothing was happening. *To Schweyk, when Baloun has gone back to his table:* What sort of meat is this?

SCHWEYK *reproachfully:* Mrs Kopecka, I'm surprised at you. *Mrs Kopecka takes the parcel out of his hand and looks into it carefully.*

SCHWEYK *at the sight of Baloun talking to the girls with huge excited gestures:* Baloun is too worked up for my liking. Put plenty of paprika in it, so it tastes like beef. It's horse. *She fixes him sternly.* All right, it's Mr Vojta's pom. I had to do it, because the Chalice'll get a bad name if one of your regulars is so hungry he has to join the Germans.

CUSTOMER AT THE BAR: Service, please!

Mrs Kopecka gives Schweyk the parcel to hold, in order to serve the customer quickly. At this moment a heavy vehicle is heard drawing up and then SS men enter, headed by Lieutenant Bullinger.

BULLINGER *to Schweyk:* Your landlady was right when she said you'd be in the pub. *To the SS men:* Clear a space! *To*

Schweyk, while the SS men push the other customers back:
Where've you got that dog, you swine?

SCHWEYK: Beg to report, sir, it said in the newspaper the dog had been stolen. Didn't you see it?

BULLINGER: Ah, taking the mickey, are you?

SCHWEYK: Beg to report sir, no sir. I only wanted to suggest you read the papers, otherwise you might miss something and then not be able to take drastic measures about it.

BULLINGER: I don't know why I stand here listening to you, it's sheer perversity on my part, I probably just want to see how far a character like you will go before he's hanged.

SCHWEYK: Yes, lieutenant, that's why, and because you want the dog.

BULLINGER: You admit you wrote me a letter asking 200 crowns for the dog?

SCHWEYK: Lieutenant Bullinger, sir, I admit that I wanted the 200 crowns, because I should have had expenses if the dog hadn't been stolen.

BULLINGER: We'll have something more to say about that at Gestapo headquarters. *To the SS men:* Search the whole place for a pomeranian dog. *Exit an SS man.*

Off stage furniture can be heard being overturned, things being broken, etc. Schweyk waits in philosophic calm, his parcel under his arm.

SCHWEYK *suddenly:* They keep quite a good slivovitz here too. *An SS man bumps against a little man as he goes past. As the latter steps back he treads on a woman's foot and says 'I beg your pardon', whereupon the SS man turns round, knocks him down with his truncheon and, together with one of the other SS men, drags him off at a nod from Bullinger. Then the SS man who has been searching comes back with Mrs Kopecka.*

SS MAN: House searched, sir. No dog found.

BULLINGER *to Mrs Kopecka:* This is a nice little hornet's nest of subversive activity you're passing off as a pub. But I shall smoke it out.

SCHWEYK: Yes indeed sir, Heil Hitler. Otherwise we might get too big for our boots and say to hell with the regulations. Mrs Kopecka, you must run your pub in such a way that everything is as transparent and clear as the water of a running spring, like Chaplain Vejvoda said when he . . .

BULLINGER: Silence, swine. I'm thinking of taking you along with me and closing your establishment down, Mrs Koscheppa!

BRETTSCHNEIDER *who has appeared at the door:* Lieutenant Bullinger, may I have a private word with you?

BULLINGER: I don't know what we could have to discuss. You know what I think you are.

BRETTSCHNEIDER: It concerns new information with regard to the whereabouts of the Vojta dog, which we have received at Gestapo headquarters and which should interest you, Lieutenant Bullinger.

The two men go into a corner and begin to gesticulate wildly. Brettschneider seems to imply that Bullinger has the dog, he seems to say 'me?' and to get angry, etc. Mrs Kopecka has returned indifferently to rinsing her glasses. Schweyk stands there in amiable unconcern. Then unfortunately, Baloun starts a successful attempt to get his parcel. At a sign from him a customer takes it from Schweyk and passes it on. It reaches Baloun, who turns it round in his hands recklessly. An SS man has been watching the parcel's peregrinations with some interest.

SS MAN: Hey, what's going on there?

In a couple of strides he reaches Baloun and takes the parcel away from him.

SS MAN *handing the parcel to Bullinger:* Sir, this parcel was just being smuggled to one of the customers, that man there, sir.

BULLINGER *opens the parcel:* Meat. Owner step forward.

SS MAN *to Baloun:* You there! You were opening the parcel.

BALOUN *troubled:* It was pushed into my hands. It don't belong to me.

BULLINGER: So it don't belong to you, don't it? Ownerless meat, apparently. *Suddenly shouting:* Then why were you opening it?

SCHWEYK *when Baloun can find no answer to this:* Beg to report,

Lieutenant Bullinger, that this stupid fellow must be innocent because he'd never have looked inside the parcel if it had been his as he'd already have known what was in it.

BULLINGER *to Baloun:* Where did you get it from?

SS MAN *when Baloun again does not reply:* I first noticed that man—*pointing to the customer who took the parcel from Schweyk* —passing the parcel along.

BULLINGER: Where did you get it?

CUSTOMER *unhappily:* It was pushed into my hands, I don't know who did it.

BULLINGER: This pub seems to be a branch of the black market. *To Brettschneider:* You were just sticking your neck out on the landlady's behalf, if I'm not mistaken, Mr Brettschneider.

MRS KOPECKA *steps forward:* Gentlemen, there are no black market deals going on at the Chalice.

BULLINGER: No? *He slaps her across the face,* I'll show you whether there are, you dirty Czech bitch.

BRETTSCHNEIDER *excitedly:* I must ask you not to judge Mrs Kopecka without a hearing. I know her to be quite uninterested in politics.

MRS KOPECKA *very pale:* I won't stand for being hit.

BULLINGER: What's this? Contradicting me? *Slaps her again.* Take her away!

Since Mrs Kopecka now tries to attack Bullinger the SS man hits her over the head.

BRETTSCHNEIDER *bending over Mrs Kopecka as she lies on the ground:* You'll have to answer for that, Bullinger. You won't manage to distract attention from the Vojta dog that way.

SCHWEYK *stepping forward:* Beg to report, I can explain everything. The parcel doesn't belong to anybody here. I know, because I put it down myself.

BULLINGER: So it was you, was it?

SCHWEYK: It belonged to a man who gave it me to keep an eye on while he went to the gents, at least that's what he said. He was about medium height with a fair beard.

BULLINGER *astonished at this unlikely story:* Tell me, are you soft in the head?

SCHWEYK *looking at him straight and seriously in the eye:* I already told you I was. I've been officially declared an idiot by a board. That's why I was kicked out of voluntary war work too.

BULLINGER: But you're bright enough for the black market, is that it? When I get you back to headquarters you'll find a hundred certificates are bugger all use to you.

SCHWEYK *submissively:* Beg to report, sir, that I quite realize they'll be bugger all use to me, because I've been landing in this sort of a mess ever since I was a kid, when all the time I've meant well and tried to do whatever they wanted. Like the time in Lubova when I was going to help the caretaker's wife at the school there to hang out her washing, if you'd come out into the passage I could tell you what happened. I got into the black market same way as Pontius Pilate got in the creed, a bit of an accident you might say.

BULLINGER *staring at him:* I just don't know why I listen to you at all, and this is the second time too. Maybe because I've never seen as big a crook before and the sight hypnotizes me.

SCHWEYK: I suppose it's like if you suddenly saw a lion in Charles Street, where you don't usually come across them, or like the time in Chotebor when the postman caught his wife with the caretaker and stabbed her. He went straight to the police to give himself up, and when they asked him what he did afterwards he said that as he came out of the house he saw a man going round the corner stark naked, so they let him go, thinking he was soft in the head, but two months later it came out that just at that time a lunatic had escaped from the asylum there without any clothes on. They didn't believe the postman even though it was the truth.

BULLINGER *astonished:* I keep on listening to you. I can't drag myself away. I know what you're thinking—that the Third Reich will last a year perhaps, or maybe ten years—

but let me tell you we're likely to be here for 10,000 years, put that in your pipe and smoke it.

SCHWEYK: You've come to stay then, as the sexton said when the landlady of the Swan married him and dropped her teeth in a tumbler for the night.

BULLINGER: Do you piss white or do you piss yellow?

SCHWEYK *amiably*: Beg to report, I piss yellowy-white, lieutenant, sir.

BULLINGER: And now you're coming along with me, even if certain people—*pointing to Brettschneider*—are ready to stick out their neck for you so far they catch it in a noose.

SCHWEYK: Very good, sir. Order must prevail. The black market's a bad thing and won't stop till there's nothing left to sell. Then we'll have order, right?

BULLINGER: And we shall get the dog too.

Exit Bullinger with the parcel under his arm. The SS men seize Schweyk and lead him off.

SCHWEYK *good-naturedly, on leaving:* I only hope you won't be disappointed when you do. A lot of my customers, when they get a dog they've been particularly keen on and have turned the place upside down for, they don't much care for it any more.

BRETTSCHNEIDER *to Mrs Kopecka, who has come to again:* Mrs Kopecka, you are the victim of certain conflicts between certain factions of the Gestapo and the SS, enough said. However, consider yourself under my protection, I shall be back shortly to discuss the matter with you in private. *Exit.*

MRS KOPECKA *staggering back to the bar, where she ties a drying cloth around her bleeding forehead:* Anyone like a beer?

KATI *looking at Schweyk's hat, which is still hanging over the table where the regulars sit:* They didn't even let him take his hat.

CUSTOMER: He'll not come back alive.

Enter young Prochazka, sheepishly. He is horrified to see Mrs Kopecka's blood-stained bandage.

YOUNG PROCHAZKA: What happened to you, Mrs Kopecka? I saw the SS driving away—was it the SS?

CUSTOMERS: They hit her over the head with a truncheon

because they said the Chalice was mixed up in the black market.—Even Mr Brettschneider of the Gestapo spoke up for her, or else she'd have been arrested.—They've taken one fellow away.

MRS KOPECKA: Mr Prochazka, the Chalice is no place for you. Only true Czechs come here.

YOUNG PROCHAZKA: Honestly, Mrs K., I've felt terrible since I last saw you, and I've learned my lesson. Can't you give me a chance to make up for it?

Mrs Kopecka's icy look makes him shudder, and he creeps out, crushed.

KATI: The SS are jumpy too because yesterday they pulled another SS man out of the Moldau with a hole in his left side.

ANNA: They throw enough Czechs in.

CUSTOMER: And all because they're having a bad time of it in the East.

FIRST CUSTOMER *to Baloun:* Wasn't that your friend they took away?

BALOUN *bursting into tears:* It's my fault. It all comes from my gluttony. Time and again I've asked the Virgin Mary to give me strength and shrivel up my stomach somehow, but it's no use. I've got my best friend in such a mess they'll probably shoot him tonight, and if not he can thank his stars and it'll be first thing tomorrow.

MRS KOPECKA *putting a slivovitz in front of him:* Drink that. Crying won't help.

BALOUN: Bless you. I've broken things up between you and your young man, and you'll not find a better one, it's only that he's weak. If I'd made the vow you asked me to maybe it wouldn't all look so black. If only I could make it now, but can I? On an empty stomach? Oh God, where will it all end?

MRS KOPECKA *goes back to the bar and begins to rinse glasses again:* Put a penny in the piano. I'll tell you where it will end.

A customer puts a coin in the player piano. It lights up and a

transparency shows the moon over the Moldau as it flows majestic-
ally away into the distance. As she rinses her glasses Mrs Kopecka
sings the 'Song of the Moldau':

The stones of the Moldau are stirring and shifting
In Prague lie three emperors turning to clay.
The great shall not stay great, the darkness is lifting.
The night has twelve hours, but at last comes the day.

For times have to change. All the boundless ambitions
Of those now in power will soon have been spent.
Like bloodspattered cocks they defend their positions
But times have to change, which no force can prevent.

The stones of the Moldau are stirring and shifting
In Prague lie three emperors turning to clay.
The great shall not stay great, the darkness is lifting.
The night has twelve hours, but at last comes the day.

INTERLUDE IN THE HIGHER REGIONS

Hitler and General von Bock, known as 'the Killer', in front of a map
of the Soviet Union. Both are over life size. Martial music.

VON BOCK
    Excuse me, Herr Hitler, your new offensive
    Is costing thousands of tanks, bombers and guns, and
       they're expensive.
    On top of that, men's lives: well, all the troops call me a
       bleeder
    Meaning just that I obey my leader
    But if you think Stalingrad's a pushover, I tell you you're
       mistaken.
HITLER
    Herr General von Bock, Stalingrad will be taken
    I've told all my people that we're winning.
VON BOCK
    Herr Hitler, the winter is almost beginning

Just imagine the snowdrifts soon as the blizzards blow
around here.

We would do better not to be found here . . .

HITLER

Herr von Bock, I'll round up the peoples of Europe like so
many cattle

And the *Little Man* shall salvage my battle.

Herr von Bock, you are not to let down the side.

VON BOCK

And my reinforcements?

HITLER

Will be supplied.

7

*Cell in a military prison with Czech prisoners who are waiting for
their medical. Among them Schweyk. They wait stripped to the waist,
but all are pretending to have the most pitiful illnesses. One, for
example, lies stretched out on the ground as if dying.*

A BENT MAN: I've seen my lawyer and got some very re-
assuring information. They can't put us in the army unless
we want to go. It's illegal.

MAN ON CRUTCHES: Then what are you going around bent
double for if you don't expect to be put in?

BENT MAN: Just in case.

The man on crutches laughs ironically.

DYING MAN *on the ground:* They wouldn't risk it with cripples
like us. They're unpopular enough already.

SHORT-SIGHTED MAN *triumphantly:* They say in Amster-
dam a German officer was crossing one of those things
called a gracht, a bit on edge round eleven at night, and he
asked a Dutchman what time it was. All the Dutchman did
was give him a solemn look and say 'My watch has stopped'.
He walked on unhappily and went up to another, and before

he had a chance to ask the man said he'd left his watch at home. The officer's supposed to have shot himself.

DYING MAN: He couldn't stand it. The contempt.

SCHWEYK: They don't shoot themselves as much as they shoot other people. There was a young innkeeper in Vrzlov whose wife was deceiving him with his own brother, and he punished the two of them with contempt and nothing else. He'd found a pair of her drawers in his brother's pony-cart, so he put them on the dressing table thinking it would make her ashamed. They had him certified incompetent by a local court, sold his pub and ran away together. He was right to this extent, though: his wife told a girl friend she'd felt a bit uncomfortable about taking his fur-lined winter overcoat with her.

BENT MAN: What are you here for?

SCHWEYK: Black market. They could have shot me, but the Gestapo needed me as a witness against the SS. I was helped by the quarrels among the bigshots. They pointed out to me that I'm lucky with my name, because it's Schweyk with a 'y', but if I spell it with an 'i' that makes me of German extraction and I can be conscripted.

MAN WITH CRUTCHES: They're even taking them from the long-term prisons now.

BENT MAN: Only if they're of German extraction.

MAN WITH CRUTCHES: Or voluntary German extraction, like this chap.

BENT MAN: The only hope is to be a cripple.

SHORT-SIGHTED MAN: I'm short-sighted. I'd never recognize an officer so I wouldn't be able to salute.

SCHWEYK: Then they could put you in a listening-post reporting enemy aircraft, it's even better if you're blind for that, because blind men develop very sharp hearing. There was a farmer in Socz for instance put out his dog's eyes to make it hear better. So they'll have a use for you.

SHORT-SIGHTED MAN *desperately:* I know a chimney-sweep in Brevnov—give him ten crowns and he'll give you such a temperature you'll want to jump out of the window.

BENT MAN: That's nothing, in Vršovice there's a midwife'll pull your leg so far out of joint for 20 crowns that you're a cripple for the rest of your life.

MAN WITH CRUTCHES: I had mine pulled out of joint for five.

DYING MAN: I didn't have to pay anything. I've got a real strangulated hernia.

MAN WITH CRUTCHES: If you have they'll operate you in Pancrac hospital, and where'll you be then?

SCHWEYK *gaily:* Anyone listening to you lot'd think you didn't want to fight for the defence of civilization against Bolshevism.

A soldier comes in and busies himself with the bucket.

SOLDIER: You've mucked up this bucket again. You can't even shit properly, you foul lot.

SCHWEYK: We were just speaking of Bolshevism. Do you people know what Bolshevism is? The sworn accomplice of Wall Street that's determined on our destruction under the leadership of the Jew Rosenfelt in the White House? *The soldier keeps fiddling with the bucket in order to hear more, so Schweyk goes on calmly:* But they don't know what they're up against. Do you know the song about the gunner of Przemysl in the First World War, when we were fighting the Czar? *He sings:*

He stood beside his gun
And just kept loading on.
He stood beside his gun
And just kept loading on
When a bullet very neatly
Cut his hands away completely.
He didn't turn a hair
Just kept on standing there.
He stood there by his gun
And just kept loading on.

The Russians are only fighting because they have to. They've no agriculture, because they've turned out the big landowners, and their industry's hamstrung by their mania

for levelling down and because the more thoughtful
workers resent the managers' high salaries. In other words
there's nothing to beat, and once we've beaten it the
Americans will have missed the boat. Am I right?

SOLDIER: Shut up, Conversation's not allowed.

He goes off angrily with the bucket.

DYING MAN: I think you're an informer.

SCHWEYK *cheerfully:* Informer, me? No. It's just that I listen
to the German radio regularly. You ought to try it, it's a
scream.

DYING MAN: It's not. It's a disgrace.

SCHWEYK *firmly:* It's a scream.

SHORT-SIGHTED MAN: That doesn't mean you have to
arsecrawl to them though.

SCHWEYK *didactically:* Don't say that. It's an art. There's
many a little insect would be glad to crawl up a tiger. The
tiger can't get at him, and he feels pretty safe, but it's the
getting in is the problem.

BENT MAN: Don't be vulgar. It isn't a nice sight when
Czechs will put up with anything.

SCHWEYK: That's what Jaroslav Vaniek told the consump-
tive pedlar. The landlord of the Swan in Budweis, a great
ox of a man, only half filled the pedlar's glass, and when the
poor wreck said nothing Vaniek turned to him and said
'Why d'you stand for that, you're as much to blame as he
is'. The pedlar just sloshed Vaniek a fourpenny one, that
was all. And now I'm going to ring the bell and get them to
get a move on with their war, my time's valuable. *Stands up.*

LITTLE FAT MAN *who has so far been sitting to one side:* You are
not to ring that bell.

SCHWEYK: Why not?

LITTLE FAT MAN *authoritatively:* Because things are moving
quite fast enough for us.

DYING MAN: Very true. Why did they pull you in?

LITTLE FAT MAN: Because my dog was stolen.

SCHWEYK *interested:* It wasn't a pom, was it?

LITTLE FAT MAN: What do you know about it?

SCHWEYK: I bet your name's Vojta. I'm very pleased to meet you. *He offers his hand, which the fat man ignores.* I'm Schweyk, I don't suppose that means anything to you, but you can shake my hand, I bet you're not pro-German any more now they've got you in here.

LITTLE FAT MAN: I accused the SS of having stolen my dog, on the evidence of one of my servants, is that good enough for you?

SCHWEYK: Quite good enough. Back in Budweis there was a teacher who had a down on one of his pupils and this pupil accused him of having a newspaper on the music stand while he was playing the organ in church. He was very religious and his wife had a lot to put up with because he had stopped her wearing short skirts, but after that they twitted him and teased him so much that in the end he said he'd even stopped believing in the Marriage at Cana. You'll march off to the Caucasus all right and shit on old Hitler, only like the landlord of the Swan said it all depends where you shit on what.

LITTLE FAT MAN: If you're called Schweyk there was a fellow who pushed up to me, a young man, as I was being brought in at the gate. He just managed to say 'Ask for Mr Schweyk' and then they got the gate open. He must still be standing around down there.

SCHWEYK: I'll have a look. I've kept expecting that one morning there'd be a little bunch of people waiting outside the prison, the landlady from the Chalice, she wouldn't want to be left out, and maybe a big fat man, all waiting for Schweyk, and no Schweyk there for them. Help me up, one of you fellows. *He goes to the little cell window and climbs on the back of the man with the crutches to look out.*

It's young Prochazka. I don't think he'll be able to see me. Give me your crutches.

He gets them and waves them around. Then young Prochazka evidently sees him and Schweyk makes himself understood with broad gestures. He outlines a fat man with a beard—Baloun—and makes the gesture of stuffing food into one's mouth and carrying

*something under one's arm. Then he gets down off the man's
back.*

What you just saw me doing probably surprised you. We
had a gentlemen's agreement, that was what he came for, I
always felt he was a decent type. I was just repeating what
he was saying, with all that business, so he'd see I'd got it.
He probably wanted me to be able to march off to Russia
with nothing on my mind.

*Commands are heard outside, and marching feet, then a military
band begins to play the Horst Wessel march.*

DYING MAN: What's going on? Did you see anything?

SCHWEYK: There's a crowd of people at the gate. Probably a
battalion marching out.

BENT MAN: That's a dreadful tune.

SCHWEYK: I think it's nice, it's sad yet it's got a swing to it.

MAN ON CRUTCHES: We'll soon be hearing it a lot more.
They play the Horst Wessel march whenever they can.
Some pimp wrote it. I'd like to know what the words
mean.

LITTLE FAT MAN: I can translate it for you. The banner
high / And tightly closed the columns / Storm troops march
on with firm and steady tread. / The comrades who have
shed their heroes' blood before us / March on with us in
spirit straight ahead.

SCHWEYK: I know a different version, we used to sing it at
the Chalice. *He sings to the accompaniment of the military band,
singing the chorus to the tune and the verses to the drumming in
between:*

Led by the drummer the
Sheep trot in bleating.
Their skins make the drumskin
Which he is beating.
  The butcher calls. They don't see where he's leading
  But march like sheep with firm and steady tread.
  The sheep before them in the slaughterhouse lie bleeding
  And march in spirit once their body's dead.

They hold up their hands to show
The work that they do
Hands that are stained with blood
And empty too.
    The butcher calls. They don't see where he's leading
    But march like sheep with firm and steady tread.
    The sheep before them in the slaughterhouse lie bleeding
    And march in spirit once their body's dead.

The crosses that go before
On big blood-red banners
Are angled to twist the poor
Like bloody great spanners.
    The butcher calls. They don't see where he's leading
    But march like sheep with firm and steady tread.
    The sheep before them in the slaughterhouse lie bleeding
    And march in spirit once their body's dead.

The other prisoners have joined in the second and third choruses. At the end the cell door opens and a German military doctor appears.

DOCTOR: Nice of you all to join in the singing so merrily. You'll be pleased to know that I consider you all healthy enough to join the army, and that you're hereby enlisted. Stand up, the lot of you, and put your shirts on. Ready to move off in ten minutes. *Exit.*

The prisoners, crushed, put their shirts on again.

BENT MAN: Without a medical examination it's completely illegal.

DYING MAN: I've got cancer of the stomach, I can prove it.

SCHWEYK *to the little fat man:* They'll put us in different units, I'm told, so we're not together and can't start buggering about. All the best, Mr Vojta, pleased to meet you, and see you all again in the Chalice at six o'clock after the war.

Schweyk, greatly moved, shakes everyone's hand as the cell door opens again. He marches out first, smartly.

SCHWEYK: Heitler! On to Moscow!

8

*Weeks later. Deep in the wintry Russian steppes Hitler's good
soldier Schweyk is marching to join his unit in the Stalingrad area. He
is muffled up in a huge pile of clothes on account of the cold.*

SCHWEYK *sings:*

When we marched off to Jaromiř
Believe it, you folks, or not
We reached the town at suppertime
And got there on the dot.
A German patrol challenges him.

FIRST SOLDIER: Halt! Password!

SCHWEYK: 'Blitzkrieg!' Could you tell me the way to Stalingrad, I've got accidentally separated from my draft and I've
been marching all day.
The first soldier examines his army papers.

SECOND SOLDIER *passing his flask:* Where are you from?

SCHWEYK: Budweis.

SOLDIER: Then you're a Czech.

SCHWEYK *nods:* I've heard things aren't too good up at the
front. *The two soldiers look at each other and laugh grimly.*

FIRST SOLDIER: What would a Czech be looking for up
there?

SCHWEYK: I'm not looking for anything, I'm coming to help
protect civilization against Bolshevism just like you, or else
it'll be a bullet in the guts, am I right?

FIRST SOLDIER: You could be a deserter.

SCHWEYK: Not me, because you'd shoot me on the spot for
breaking my oath as a soldier and not dying for my Führer,
Heil Hitler.

SECOND SOLDIER: So you're one of the keen ones, are you?
Takes his flask back.

SCHWEYK: I'm as keen as Tonda Novotny when he applied
at the vicarage in Vysocany for the job of sexton not knowing if the church was protestant or Catholic, and because the

vicar was in his braces and there was a woman in the room
he said he was a protestant and got it wrong for a start.

FIRST SOLDIER: And why must it be Stalingrad of all places,
you doubtful ally?

SCHWEYK: Because that's where my regimental office is,
mate, where I've got to get my papers stamped to show I've
reported, otherwise they're bugger all use and I shan't be
able to show my face in Prague again. Heil Hitler!

FIRST SOLDIER: And suppose we said to you 'Sod Hitler!'
and we're deserting to the Russians and taking you with us
because you can speak Russian, because Czech is supposed
to be like it.

SCHWEYK: Czech's very like it, but I'd say you'd do better
not to, I don't know my way around here and I'd sooner get
directions to Stalingrad.

FIRST SOLDIER: Perhaps you'd rather not trust us—is that
the reason?

SCHWEYK: I'd rather think you were good soldiers. Because
if you were deserting you'd be bound to be taking something with you for the Russians, a machine-gun or something, maybe a good telescope, something they could use,
and you'd hold it up in front of you so they wouldn't shoot
you at sight. That's the way it's done, I'm told.

FIRST SOLDIER *laughs:* You mean they'll understand that
even if it isn't Russian. I get you, you're a crafty bastard.
And you'd sooner say you just want to know where your
grave at Stalingrad is. It's that way. *He shows him.*

SECOND SOLDIER: And if anyone asks you, we're a military
patrol and we gave you the full treatment, got that?

FIRST SOLDIER *as he goes:* And that's not bad advice of
yours, mate.

SCHWEYK *waving after them:* Glad to help. Be seeing you.
*The soldiers move off quickly. Schweyk too continues in the direction
he was shown, but he can be seen to be wandering from it in a wide
arc. He vanishes into the gloom. When he reappears on the other
side he stops for a short time at a signpost and reads: 'Stalingrad—
50 km.' He shakes his head and marches on. The moving clouds in*

the sky are now red from distant fires. He looks at them interestedly as he marches.

SCHWEYK *sings:*

When Hitler sent for me
To help him win his war
I thought the whole damn lark would last
A fortnight and no more.

While he continues to march, smoking his pipe, the clouds turn pale again and the regulars' table at the Chalice appears, bathed in pink light. Baloun is kneeling on the floor, next to him stands Mrs Kopecka with her embroidery, and at the table Anna is sitting behind a beer.

BALOUN *as if reciting the litany:* I now swear of my own free will and on an empty stomach, since all attempts by everybody to organize some meat for me have failed, that's to say without me having had a real meal, by the Virgin Mary and all the saints, that I will never volunteer for the Nazi army, and may Almighty God help me. I do this in memory of my friend Mr Schweyk, now marching across the icy Russian steppes faithfully doing his duty because he has to. He was a good man.

MRS KOPECKA: Right, you can stand up now.

ANNA *takes a drink from the beer mug, stands up and embraces him:* And now we can get married as soon as we've got the papers from Protivin. *After kissing him, to Mrs Kopecka:* What a pity things haven't worked out for you.

Young Prochazka stands in the doorway, a parcel under his arm.

MRS KOPECKA: Mr Prochazka, I forbade you ever to set foot in here again. It's all over between us. Since your great love doesn't even stretch to two pounds of pickled pork.

YOUNG PROCHAZKA: What if I've brought it, though? *Shows his parcel.* Two pounds of pickled pork.

MRS KOPECKA: What, you've brought it? In spite of what you might get if they caught you?

ANNA: It's not really necessary any more, is it? Mr Baloun has taken his oath without.

MRS KOPECKA: But you must admit it proves a genuine

affection on Mr Prochazka's part. Rudolf! *She embraces him ardently.*

ANNA: That would please Mr Schweyk if he knew about it, poor old fellow. *She looks tenderly at Schweyk's bowler, which is hanging over the regulars' table.* Take good care of that hat, Mrs Kopecka, I'm certain Mr Schweyk will be back to collect it after the war.

BALOUN *sniffing the parcel:* Some lentils would go well with that.

The Chalice disappears again. From upstage staggers a drunk in two thick sheepskins and a steel helmet. Schweyk encounters him.

DRUNK: Halt! Who are you? I can see you're one of our lot and not a gorilla, thank God. I'm Chaplain Ignatius Bullinger from Metz, you don't happen to have a drop of kirsch with you, do you?

SCHWEYK: Beg to report I haven't.

CHAPLAIN: That's odd. I don't want it for boozing, as you may have thought, you swine, admit it, that's what you think of your priest; I need it for my car with the field altar back there, I've run out of petrol, they're keeping the Lord short of petrol in Rostov, they're going to have to answer for that all right when they stand before the throne of God and He asks in a voice like thunder 'You motorized My altar, but what about the petrol?'

SCHWEYK: I don't know, your Reverence. Could you tell me which is the way to Stalingrad?

CHAPLAIN: God knows. Do you know the one about the bishop who asks the ship's captain in a storm 'Are we going to make it?', and the captain answers 'We're in God's hands now, bishop', and the bishop just says 'As bad as that?' and bursts into tears?

SCHWEYK: Is Lieutenant Bullinger of the SS your brother, sir?

CHAPLAIN: Yes, for my sins. D'you know him? So you've no kirsch or vodka?

SCHWEYK: No, and you'll catch cold if you sit down in the snow.

CHAPLAIN: It doesn't matter about me. But they're mean with their petrol, they'll see how they get along without God and without the Word of God in battle. By land, sea and air, and so on. I only joined their stupid Nazi Union for German Christians after the most terrible struggles with my conscience. For their sake I've scrapped Jesus the Jew and made him a Christian in my sermons, with lots of bull about his blue eyes and references to Wotan, and I tell them the world has got to be German, even if it costs rivers of blood, because I'm a worm, a wretched apostate worm who's betrayed his beliefs for pay, and they go and give me too little petrol and just look what they've brought me to.

SCHWEYK: The Russian steppes, chaplain, and you'd better come back to Stalingrad with me and sleep it off. *He pulls him to his feet and drags him along a few yards.* You'll have to walk on your own feet, though, or I'll leave you lying here, I've got to find my draft and come to Hitler's rescue.

CHAPLAIN: I can't leave my field altar standing here or it'll be captured by the Bolsheviks, and what then? They're heathens. I came past a cottage just over there, the chimney was smoking, d'you think they'd have any vodka, just tap them on the head with your rifle butt and Bob's your uncle. Are you a German Christian?

SCHWEYK: No, the ordinary sort. Now don't start being sick over yourself, it'll freeze on you.

CHAPLAIN: Freeze? I'm as cold as the devil. I'll hot things up for them at Stalingrad, though.

SCHWEYK: You've got to get there first.

CHAPLAIN: I've no real confidence left any more. *Calmly, almost soberly:* You know, What's-his-name, they laugh at me to my face, me the priest of God, when I threaten them with hell. The only explanation I can see is that they think they're there already. Religion's going to pieces, and it's Hitler who's responsible, don't tell anybody I said so.

SCHWEYK: Hitler's a wet fart, I'm telling you because you're drunk. And who's responsible for Hitler, them that handed him Czechoslovakia on a plate at Munich for 'peace in our time', and a fat long time it was too. But the war's lasted all right, and for a lot of people it's been 'war in our time' from what I can see.

CHAPLAIN: So you're against the war that has to be fought against the godless Bolsheviks, you swine. D'you know I'm going to have you shot when we get to Stalingrad?

SCHWEYK: If you don't pull yourself together and get a move on you'll never get there. I'm not against war, and I'm not walking to Stalingrad just for a lark, but because like Naczek the cook said back in the First World War 'Get near the shooting, you'll find something cooking'.

CHAPLAIN: Don't give me that. You're saying to yourself 'They can stuff their war', I can see it from your face. *Grabs him.* What do you want to be pro-war for, what do you get out of it, confess it means bugger all to you.

SCHWEYK *roughly:* I'm marching to Stalingrad, and you are too, because it's orders and we'd probably starve here left to ourselves. I've told you once already.

They march on.

CHAPLAIN: War's a depressing business on foot. *Stops.* There's that cottage, we'll go in there, got your safety-catch off?

A cottage appears, they go up to it.

SCHWEYK: But just one thing, don't kick up a row, they're people like you and me, and you've drunk enough.

CHAPLAIN: Have your finger on the trigger, they're heathens, don't answer back.

Out of the cottage come an old peasant woman, and a young woman with a little child.

CHAPLAIN: Look, they're going to run away. We've got to stop that. Ask where they've buried the vodka. And look at that shawl she's wearing, I'll have that, I'm freezing like hell.

SCHWEYK: You're freezing because you're drunk and you've got two fur coats already. *To the young woman, who stands without moving:* Good evening, which is the way to Stalingrad? *The young woman points rather absent-mindedly.*

CHAPLAIN: Does she admit they've got vodka?

SCHWEYK: You sit down, I'll deal with them and then we'll go on, I don't want any trouble. *To the woman, cordially:* Why are you standing outside the house like that? Were you just going away? *The woman nods.* That's a thin shawl you've got on, though; have you nothing else? It's not really enough, is it?

CHAPLAIN *sitting on the ground:* Use your rifle butt, they're gorillas, the lot of them. Heathens.

SCHWEYK *roughly:* You bloody well shut up. *To the woman:* Vodka? This man is ill.

Schweyk has accompanied all his questions with illustrative gestures. The woman shakes her head.

CHAPLAIN *bad-temperedly:* You shaking your head? I'll show you. Here am I freezing, and you shake your head. *He scrambles to his feet with difficulty and staggers towards the woman, his fist raised. She retreats into the cottage, closing the door after her. The chaplain kicks it in and pushes his way in.* I'll settle your hash.

SCHWEYK *who has vainly tried to hold him back:* You stay out. It's not your house. *He follows him in. The old woman goes in too. Then a scream is heard from the woman and sound of a fight. Schweyk from within:* And put that knife away. Stay still, will you! I'll break your arm, you swine. Right, outside!

Out of the cottage comes the woman with the child. She has one of the chaplain's coats on. Behind her comes the old woman.

SCHWEYK *following them into the open:* Let him sleep it off. Make sure you get well away.

OLD WOMAN *curtseys deeply to Schweyk in the old style:* God protect you, soldier, you're a good man, and if we had any bread left I'd give you a crust. You look as if you could do with it. Which way's your road?

SCHWEYK: To Stalingrad, ma, to the battle. Could you tell me how I get there?

OLD WOMAN: You're a Slav, you speak the way we do, you haven't come to murder, you're not one of Hitler's lot, God bless you.

She begins to bless him with broad gestures.

SCHWEYK *without embarrassment:* Don't worry, ma, I'm a Slav, and don't waste your blessing on me, I'm a collaborationist.

OLD WOMAN: God shall protect you, my son, you've a pure heart, you've come to help us, you'll help beat Hitler's lot.

SCHWEYK *firmly:* No offence, I've got to get on, it's not my own choice. And I'm beginning to believe you must be deaf, ma.

OLD WOMAN *in spite of the fact that her daughter keeps tugging at her sleeve:* You'll help us to get rid of these bandits, hurry soldier, and God bless you.

The young woman pulls the old one away, and they move off. Schweyk marches on shaking his head. Night has fallen and the stars have appeared. Schweyk stops at a signpost again and turns a dark lantern on to it. Astonished he reads: 'Stalingrad—50 km' and marches on. Suddenly shots ring out. Schweyk immediately puts his hands up, holding his rifle, in order to surrender. No one comes, however, and the shots cease. Schweyk goes on more quickly. When he again appears in his circular course he is out of breath and sits down on a snowdrift.

SCHWEYK *sings:*

When we were stationed in Kovno
They couldn't have been slicker
They had the boots from off our feet
For one tiny glass of liquor.

The pipe sinks from his mouth, he dozes off and dreams. The regulars' table at the Chalice appears in golden light. Around it sit Mrs Kopecka in her bridal gown, young Prochazka in his Sunday suit, Kati, Anna and Baloun. In front of the latter is a full plate.

MRS KOPECKA: And what you're getting for the wedding breakfast, Mr Baloun, is your pickled pork. You swore without it, and that's to your credit, but a little bit of meat now and then won't hurt to help you keep your vow.

BALOUN *eating:* You know, I really do like eating. God bless it. The dear Lord created everything, from the sun down to the carraway seed. *Indicating his plate:* Can that be a sin?

Pigeons fly, chickens peck up seed from the earth. The land-lord of the Huss knew seventeen ways of cooking a chicken, five sweet, six savoury, four with stuffing. 'The earth brings forth wine for me, likewise bread, and I'm not able to use them', the minister at Budweis used to say, that wasn't allowed to eat because he had diabetes. I had a hare at the Schlossbräu in Pilsen back in 1932, the cook has died since, so people don't go there any more, and I've never had another like it. It was in gravy with dumplings. There's nothing special about that, but there was something in that gravy did things to the dumplings, quite fantastic, they'd hardly have recognized themselves, inspired they were, really first class, I've never come across anything like it again, the cook took the recipe to the grave with him. It's a real loss to mankind.

ANNA: Don't complain. What do you suppose Mr Schweyk would say about it, when he probably hasn't even got a baked potato to his name?

BALOUN: That's true, mustn't grumble. You can always manage. In Pudonice when my sister got married they had a real crowd, thirty of them, it was at the pub there, girls and chaps and the old folk too, and they kept going right through soup, veal, pork, chicken, two roast calves and two fat pigs, the lot from snout to tail, and dumplings with it and great barrels of sauerkraut, and first beer and then schnapps. All I remember is my plate was never empty and I had a bucketful of beer or a tumber of schnapps after every mouthful. At one point there was absolute silence, just like in church, that was when they brought the roast pork in. They were all such good pals together sitting there, eating their fill, I'd have gone through fire for any one of them. And there were all sorts among them, there was a judge from the County Court at Pilsen used to really have it in for the thieves and the workers when he'd got his wig on. Eating draws people's sting.

MRS KOPECKA: In honour of Mr Baloun I am now going to sing the 'Song of the Chalice'. *She sings:*

Come right in and take a seat
Join us at the table
Soup and Moldau fish to eat
Much as you are able.
>   If you need a bite of bread
>   And a roof above your head
>   You're a man and that will do.
>   The place of honour's here for you.
>   If you've 80 Hellers.

We don't want to know your life
Everyone's invited.
Step inside and bring the wife
We shall be delighted.
>   All you need's a friendly face
>   Clever talk is out of place
>   Eat your cheese and drink your beer
>   And you'll find a welcome here
>   So will 80 Hellers.

One day soon we shall begin
Looking at the weather
And we'll find the world's an inn
Where men come together.
>   All alike will come inside
>   Nobody will be denied
>   Here's a roof against the storm
>   Where the freezing can get warm
>   Even on 80 Hellers.

Everyone has joined in the refrain.

BALOUN: My grandfather used to be an accountant with the water board, and when they told him at the Pankrac clinic he'd have to cut down on his food or go blind he answered 'I've seen quite enough, but I haven't eaten enough by a long chalk'. *Suddenly stops eating.* Christ, let's hope old Schweyk isn't freezing to death out there in that icy cold.

ANNA: He mustn't lie down. It's just when you feel nice and warm that you're closest to dying of exposure, they say.

The Chalice disappears. It is daytime again. A snowstorm has set in. Schweyk moves beneath a blanket of flakes. The rattle of tank tracks becomes audible.

SCHWEYK *sitting up:* Nearly dropped off. But now, on to Stalingrad!

He works his way up and starts marching again. Then out of the driving snow a large armoured vehicle appears full of German soldiers with chalk white or blueish faces under their steel helmets, all of them wrapped up in every kind of rags, skins, even women's skirts.

THE SOLDIERS *sing the 'German Miserere':*

One day our superiors said: Germany, awaken
The small town of Danzig has got to be taken.
They gave us tanks and bombers, then Poland was invaded.
In two weeks at the outside we had made it.
God preserve us.

One day our superiors said: Germany, awaken
Now Norway and France have got to be taken.
They gave us tanks and bombers, both countries were
    invaded.
Five weeks of 1940, and we'd made it.
God preserve us.

One day our superiors said: Germany, awaken
The Balkans and Russia have got to be taken.
The third year saw the Balkans and Russia both invaded.
We should have won, but something has delayed it.
God preserve us.

Wait till our superiors say: Germany, awaken
The depths of the ocean and the moon must be taken.
Over Russia's cold steppes they've left us to roam
And the fighting's tough and we don't know our way home.
God preserve us and bring us back home alive.

The armoured vehicle disappears again in the snowstorm. Schweyk marches on. A signpost appears, pointing at right angles to his

route. Schweyk ignores it. Suddenly, however, he stops and listens.
Then he bends down, whistles softly and snaps his fingers. Out of the
snow-covered undergrowth creeps a starving mongrel.

SCHWEYK: I knew you were there in the bushes, hanging
about and wondering whether to come out or not, eh?
You're a cross between a schnauzer and an alsatian, with a
bit of mastiff in the middle. I shall call you Ajax. Stop cring-
ing and cut out that shivering, I can't stand it. *He marches on,*
followed by the dog. We're going to Stalingrad. You'll find
other dogs there and plenty going on. If you want to get
through the war in one piece, keep close to the others and
stick to routine, don't volunteer for anything, lie doggo till
you get a chance to bite. War doesn't last for ever, any more
than peace does, and when it's over I'll take you along to
the Chalice and we'll have to keep an eye on Baloun to see
he doesn't eat you, Ajax. There'll still be people wanting
dogs, and pedigrees'll still have to be faked because they
want pure breeds, it's a load of tripe but that's what they
want. Don't get under my feet, or you'll get a fourpenny
one. On to Stalingrad!

The blizzard gets thicker and envelops them.

EPILOGUE

Hitler's good soldier Schweyk is marching untiringly to Stalingrad,
which remains just as far away as ever, when a wild music is heard
amidst the snowstorm and a larger-than-life figure appears: Adolf
Hitler. The historic meeting between Hitler and Schweyk takes place.

HITLER
Halt! Who goes there? Friend or foe?
SCHWEYK *giving the customary salute:*
Heitler!
HITLER *over the storm:*
I can't hear what you say.
SCHWEYK *louder:*
I said Heitler. Can you hear me now?

HITLER

Yes.

SCHWEYK

It's the wind that carries it away.

HITLER

You're right, and we seem to be getting some snow. Do you recognize me?

SCHWEYK

Beg to report, sir, no.

HITLER

I am the Führer.

Schweyk, whose hand has remained up in the Nazi salute, raises the other to join it in a gesture of surrender, dropping his gun.

SCHWEYK

Holy Saint Joseph!

HITLER

At ease. Who are you?

SCHWEYK

I'm Schweyk from Budweis at the bend in the Moldau. And I've come to help you at Stalingrad. But would you mind telling me just one thing: where is it?

HITLER

How the devil can you expect me to know any of our positions

In these blasted Bolshevistic traffic conditions?

The direct road from Rostov to Stalingrad looked no longer than my finger on the map.

It is, though;—filthy Communistic trap!

What's more, the winter's set in early again this year—on the first of November instead of the third.

It's the second year running that that's occurred.

This winter's probably all part of their damned Bolshevistic theories.

As a matter of fact at the moment I don't even know where the front or the rear is.

I set out from the principle that the stronger side would win.

SCHWEYK

That's just what's happened.

He has begun to stamp his feet and fling his arms around his chest, being extremely cold.

HITLER

Mr Schweyk, remember, if the Third Reich should cave in the forces of nature were the only thing that could hold me.

SCHWEYK

Yes, the winter and the Bolsheviks. So you've already told me.

HITLER *beginning an extended explanation:*

History shows us that East and West don't mix, and if . . .

SCHWEYK

Look, you explain it to me on the way, or else we'll be frozen stiff.

HITLER

Right. Then forward.

SCHWEYK

But which way shall we go?

HITLER

Let's try the north.

They advance a few paces to the north.

SCHWEYK *stops, sticks two fingers in his mouth and whistles to Hitler:*

That way there's some pretty deep snow.

HITLER

Then the south.

They advance a few paces southwards.

SCHWEYK *stops and whistles:*

That way there are mountains of dead men.

HITLER

Then I'll push East.

They advance eastwards a few paces.

SCHWEYK *stops and whistles:*

That way you'll find an awful lot of red men.

HITLER

You're right.

SCHWEYK

            Maybe we could go home then? That'd make
a bit of sense.

HITLER

What: and face my German people without any defence?
*Hitler rushes in each direction, one after the other. Schweyk keeps
whistling him back.*

HITLER

East! West! North! South!

SCHWEYK

You can't stay here, and you can't get out.
Hitler's movements in all directions become quicker.

SCHWEYK *begins to sing:*

Yes, you cannot retreat, and you cannot progress.
You're all rotten on top, below you're a mess.
The east wind is far too cold, and hellfire is far too hot
So they've left it to me now to say whether or not
I should heap you with shit or riddle you with shot.
Hitler's desperate attempts at escape have turned into a wild dance.

CHORUS OF ALL THE ACTORS *taking off their masks and
going down to the footlights:*

For times have to change. All the boundless ambitions
Of those now in power will soon have been spent.
Like bloodspattered cocks they defend their positions
But times have to change—which no force can prevent.

The stones of the Moldau are stirring and shifting
In Prague lie three emperors turning to clay.
The great shall not stay great, the darkness is lifting.
The night has twelve hours, but at last comes the day.

Appendix

HENRY SLEPT BESIDE HIS NEWLY WEDDED*

Henry slept beside his newly wedded
Heiress to a castle on the Rhine
Snake bites, which tormented the false lover
Would not let him peacefully recline.

At the stroke of twelve the curtain parted.
On the sill a pale cold hand appeared.
In a shroud he saw his Wilhelmina
And her mournful, ghostly voice he heard.

Do not tremble, said his Wilhelmina;
Faithless lover, do not be afraid.
I have not come here in hate or anger
I've not come to curse your marriage bed.

Bitter grief my poor young life has shortened
I have died because I loved you well
But the Lord has fortified my spirit
Saved me from the headlong plunge to hell.

Why did I believe your protestations
That your love would always be the same
Never dreaming that for you to vanquish
Maiden's heart was but a paltry game?

Do not weep. This world does not deserve it
'Tis not worth a single tear or moan.
Live serene and happy with Eliza
Now that you have got her for your own.

Henry, you have treasure, ah, uncounted
Use it now to give my soul repose.
Give your Wilhelmine the peace of spirit
You denied her living, heaven knows.

Sacrifice! cried Henry in his fever;
That's what you have come to ask, he cried.

* This street ballad is sung by Kati and Anna in scene 4. Translated
by Ralph Manheim.

Whereupon the poor spurned woman vanished
And the churl committed suicide.

God had mercy on her, but the faithless
Lover was condemned beyond repair.
Still he lives, an evil spooky monster
Wand'ring in the dreary midnight air.

Notes and Variants
to *The Visions of Simone Machard*

THE VISIONS OF SIMONE MACHARD

Texts by Brecht

Little Simone Machard works for the hostellerie at a small town called Saint-Martin in central France. She is there to help out, primarily in connection with the hotel petrol pump; the hotel also runs a transport business. It is June 1940; the Nazis have taken Paris; streams of refugees are pouring across central France and passing through Saint-Martin.

Simone's seventeen-year-old brother is at the front; she loves him dearly and is sure that he is involved in the fighting. Meanwhile in the village and in the hotel she finds that at this point, in the middle of a great national disaster, high and low alike can think of nothing but themselves. It is now that she reads a book given her by her teacher, which contains the story of the Maid of Orleans, greatest of all French patriots.

During those feverish nights, with the leading Germans already up to the Loire, she is moved by the course of events to dream that she is herself Saint Joan. An angel appears to her from the garage roof and tells her that she has been chosen to save France. He has the features of her soldier brother André. In her dream the legend of the book mingles with the reality of the little hotel. The hotel's *patron* is suddenly a *connétable* of the royal court; the hotel staff, the drivers and the old night porter, wear armour and form a little unit of feudal soldiery who escort her to the king; while in the king himself she recognizes the spineless local mayor.

Thereafter Simone at the hostellerie undergoes a miniature version of the terrible and uplifting fate of Joan of Arc, and again and again in her dreams she turns into the saint.

She dreams that the angel gives her an invisible drum. He tells her that this drum is the soil of France, and that in an emergency the soil of France—her drum—will resound, summoning the people to resist France's enemies. In her role as a great popular leader she then in her dream goes to the king, holds confidential talks with the king-mayor and warns him not to spend his time playing cards with his nobles, the *patron-connétable* and the other luminaries of Saint-Martin, but instead to attend to the arming and feeding of the people. The people, for their part, are called on to fight wholeheartedly. In this way she manages to unite king, people and nobles and to crown the king-mayor in Rheims.

In the real world of the hotel, when the *patron* and his drivers simply wish to run away from the Germans, she fetches the mayor and has the hotel forced to hand over its stocks of food to the municipality rather than remove them to the interior, while the drivers and their lorries are made to evacuate the refugees who are blocking the French army from using the roads.

(The *patron* allows the child to have her way because at least this stops his hostellerie from being looted, and the drivers help her because they sympathize with her anxiety for her brother at the front.)

But when she calls for the hostellerie's secret stocks of petrol to be destroyed to prevent them from falling into enemy hands she is going too far, and the *patron*'s mother dismisses her.

That night she dreams the chapter in her book in which the Maid, following her initial victories, encounters the first problems in her own ranks. Although Paris is still in enemy hands she is not given command of a fresh army. The king-mayor and the *patron-connétable* ennoble her, admittedly, but they take away her sword. Once more the angel appears on the garage roof and she has to tell him that she has been dismissed. Severely the angel recommends her to stick to her course and not, for instance, to let the petrol fall into the hands of the Germans, or else their murderous tanks will be able to keep on thrusting ahead.

A few days later the Germans enter Saint-Martin. The

patron has fled. His mother and old Captain Beleire, a Laval supporter and vineyard owner, wish to come to terms with the victorious Germans at any price. To prove that they mean to collaborate they tell the German commandant that the petrol is hidden in the brickworks. But the brickworks is already ablaze when the Germans get there. Simone has set fire to it. This act of sabotage threatens the new and promising Franco-German collaboration. Wanted: the incendiarist.

In a disturbing dream Simone once again encounters the heroic Joan of the legend, now deserted by her own side, because the Queen Mother Isabeau and the Duke of Burgundy have asserted themselves at Court and are trying to arrange an armistice with the enemy. The Queen Mother looks just like the mother of the *patron*, while the Duke of Burgundy is like the *connétable*. Only Simone, now wide awake, cannot believe this dream. And when on the *patron*'s return he feels sorry for her, and he and the drivers want to take her away, she insists on staying. How is her brother to find her if and when he returns? So she is denounced to the Germans and arrested.

In a final vision Simone dreams that she, Joan, has been taken captive and handed over by the enemy to an ecclesiastical court which has to decide whether the voices which she heard summoning her to resist the enemy came in fact from God or from the devil. She is tragically shocked to find that the noble judges who condemn her to the stake for having spoken with the devil's voice only are all people whom she knows: the mayor, the Captain, the *patron*, with the *patron*'s mother putting the case for the prosecution.

Simone dreams this last dream in prison, and the following morning the Germans hand her back to the French. Her friends among the hotel staff are hopeful for her. They feel that a French official inquiry into the fire must be bound to admit the patriotic nature of her motives. But there are good reasons why the German attitude should be so generous. The Germans think it undesirable that there should have been an act of sabotage which might act as a precedent for others.

And shooting a child would jeopardize the collaboration they so badly need. So they have agreed with their French friends that the case should be sidetracked.

Simone has to hear the *patron* and his mother, her employers, giving evidence against her, while the mayor leaves her to her fate. Numb with shock, she learns that a French court finds that her action was not undertaken for patriotic reasons, but that she caused the fire for purely personal motives, as a mischievous act of revenge for her dismissal. She is sent for corrective training.

The people, however, are not fooled. When the *patron* returns to the hostellerie he finds that his staff have left. And as Simone is being led away after the verdict Saint-Martin is shaken by a bombing attack. English planes are carrying on the struggle.

For Simone these explosions have a special meaning. Did her dream angel not tell her that the soil of France was her invisible drum, whose sound would bring the sons of France hurrying to defend it? And here is French soil reverberating. It is the angel, her brother André, who has sent her the planes. (N.B.: Interwoven with the play is the delicate story of little Simone's relations with a wounded soldier, one of her brother's friends.)

[GW *Schriften zum Theater* 3, pp. 1181–5. This plan for the play, which may have been conceived as a film treatment, differs from our text, particularly in its ending, which is unlike that in any other version. Nowhere else is the Captain specifically described as being old, while the identification of the drum with the soil of France is also unusually clearly made. Note that there is no mention of the refugees in the gymnasium.]

WORKING PLAN

1. *the germans invade france. at the hostellerie 'au relais' it is business as usual, but simone machard is reading a book of legends.*

(a) two drivers see bombs, an old man mends tyres, a soldier licks his wounds, a child reads a book.

(b) the colonel does not wish to be greeted.

(c) conversation about the treachery of the top people, about visions, hordes of refugees, headaches, teachers and wine.

(d) soldiers get their dixie half-filled with lentils. simone's brother is unknown.

(e) the *patron* defends his stocks and tells simone to give the colonel his bill.

(f) the hotel has a star, the staff remain cool.

(g) the mayor is bawled out by the colonel because the roads are blocked.

(h) the mayor wants lorries for the refugees, the *patron* has no petrol, the staff confirm it, the captain needs the lorries for his barrels of wine, the war is lost.

(i) only a miracle can save france, in the mayor's view; the staff say 'simone thinks one will take place'.

2. *joan of arc, summoned by divine voices, crowns the king in rheims and unites all frenchmen against the hereditary foe.*

(a) the angel calls joan and gives her the task.

(b) she gets helmet and bayonet.

(c) the ajaxes escort her, and battles are won.

(d) she recognizes the king.

(e) her argument with the king.

(f) she crowns him.

3. *simone gets a hearing for the mayor, and the hotel is saved.*

(a) the germans have crossed the loire, the staff has breakfast, the *patron* has certain wishes, the staff has breakfast, simone disappears.

(b) the *patron* is horrified to find that he is not liked. simone is looked for by her parents.

(c) the mayor arrives with soldiers, having been fetched by simone. the lorries are requisitioned but the mayor weakens.

(*d*) simone supports him and arranges everything, aided by madame mère. the soldiers are given wine, and leave for the front. the village is given the food stocks, and simone's parents are the first.

(*e*) the wave of patriotism infects the *patron*. handshake and toast. the petrol must be saved, as simone said.

(*f*) the *patron* has departed. madame mère fires simone. the mayor admires the tip.

4. *joan, rewarded by the court but dismissed in her native village, is encouraged by her voices to continue the struggle.*

(*a*) although the enemy is still in her country, joan can get no more troops.

(*b*) instead she is thanked for her services. she is knighted with her own sword.

(*c*) but her sword is not returned to her; the king gives it to the connétable as a mark of gratitude.

(*d*) the angel appears and tells her to carry on the struggle.

5. *the germans occupy the village. simone sets fire to the petrol.*

(*a*) madame mère receives the german commandant. 'he's human like the rest of us'.

(*b*) the captain harangues the staff. in future discipline will prevail.

(*c*) simone hears the captain warning the mayor not to conceal the existence of the petrol in the brickworks.

(*d*) simone tells the mayor of her plan to set fire to the brickworks. he seems to approve.

(*e*) the opponents also get on at a low level. the commandant's batman talks with the wounded soldier.

(*f*) the gentry enter the yard to inspect the brickworks. a good understanding prevails.

(*g*) the brickworks are ablaze.

6. *simone is surrendered by the top people.*

(*a*) simone's parents come to thank her: as a result of her generous action her father has got the job with the council.

(*b*) the *patron* returns. he is embarrassed by the parents' tributes: 'your hotel is france in miniature'. père gustave accompanies him inside.

daydream

(*a*) the maid's messenger is kept from the king. why?

(*b*) because the english are within. and what is being talked about?

(*c*) the maid. and what else?

(*d*) the fact that she is to blame for the war.

(*e*) so she isn't relieved, but her troops are thrown in again. and so she is captured.

(*f*) but the angel appears once more and assures her that everything she did was right, and warns her to stick to her mission.

6. *simone is surrendered by the top people*, continued.

(*c*) the drivers urge simone to flee. she stands by her faith in the *patron*.

(*d*) then the *patron* comes out too and urges her to flee.

(*e*) simone is seized by panic, and does flee.

(*f*) the german commandant and the french gentry enter the yard and a search is made for simone. she is not there. the commandant is angry and goes back indoors.

(*g*) sigh of relief from the gentry. simone is standing in the yard. she has come back. they implore her. she refuses to flee. the commandant arrives. simone: it's me.

7. *the english hand joan over to an ecclesiastical court consisting of frenchmen, which interrogates her about the angel.*

(*a*) the english bring joan before the ecclesiastical court. they ask for a report as to whether the voices come from god or from the devil.

(*b*) the connétable, the burgundian and the renegade colonel don their ecclesiastical robes.

(*c*) the ecclesiastical court discusses the voices' origin with joan and finds them devilish.

8. *trial of simone machard by the authorities of her village. she is found not guilty of the crime of sabotage but is sent to the pious sisters' corrective institution on the grounds of incendiarism and vindictiveness.*

(a) the germans hand simone back.

(b) the commission goes out of its way to whitewash her of any accusation of sabotaging the germans.

(c) the staff welcome this attitude on the court's part and hope for her release.

(d) the remainder of the hearing is devoted to simone's attitude to her employers, particularly on the day of the great panic.

(e) questioned about her motives for incendiarism she continues to insist that she did it for france's sake.

(f) she is forced however to admit that she really wanted to save the petrol from its owners.

(g) she is therefore handed over to the pious sisters of sainte-madeleine for correction.

(h) while she says good-bye in the yard to the staff and to her parents the commission goes off to report to the german commandant.

> [BBA 1204/1–3. This is one of the most elaborately worked out of all Brecht's characteristic structural plans. It is mounted on card, with scenes 1–8 (and their sub-headings) forming eight parallel columns. There are pencilled figures by Brecht giving (apparently) the estimated duration of each sub-scene, and it seems altogether probable that the collaborators used it as a basis for their first script.]

THE DREAMS

The dreams in which Simone relives the St Joan legend can be made intelligible to audiences unaware of the legend by the large-scale projection of individual pages from the book, possibly including woodcut illustrations.

For the *first dream*: 'Summoned by an angel to save France,

Joan units the French by crowning Charles VII king in the city of Rheims.'

For the *second dream*: 'Following some brilliant victories, Joan is ennobled. However, she has powerful enemies at court who would like to see an armistice.'

For the *third dream*: 'Betrayed into enemy hands, Joan is handed over to an ecclesiastical court which condemns her to death.'

> [GW *Schriften zum Theater* 3, p. 1185. These captions can be compared with those in the plans quoted in the Editorial Note, below. Illustrations reproduced from old illuminated manuscripts are gummed into one or two of Brecht's typescripts of the play.]

FIRST DREAM OF SIMONE MACHARD (DURING THE NIGHT OF 14/15 JUNE)

I was addressed from the garage roof in a loud voice as 'Joan!', went immediately out into the yard and saw *the angel* on the roof of the garage. He waved to me in friendly fashion and told me that I had been called to defeat France's enemies. He ordered me to go straightway to Châlons and crown the king, as I had read in the book. After the angel had disappeared once more the soldier came out of the garage towards me and handed me sword and helmet. The former looked like a bayonet. I asked whether I should clean it for him but he answered that it was against the enemies of France. Thereupon I felt as if I were standing in green countryside. A strong wind was blowing and the sky was like it is between four and five in the morning when you go to mass. Then I saw how the earth, together with all the meadows and poplars upon it, curved as if it were a ball, and how the enemy loomed up in a mighty procession without end. In front rode the drummer with a voice like a wolf and his drum was stretched with a Jew's skin; a vulture perched on his shoulder with the features of Farouche the banker from Lyons. Close behind him came the Marshal Incendiarist. He went on foot, a fat clown, in seven uniforms and in none of them did he look human. Above these two devils was a canopy of newsprint, so it was easy for me to recognize them. Behind them rode the remaining executioners and marshals, with countenances for the most part like the backsides of plucked chickens, and behind them drove an endless procession of guns and tanks and railway trains, also automobiles on which were altars or torture chambers, for everything was on wheels.

> [BBA 118–19. More than anything else, this draft of the first dream, part of which was taken into the play (p. 20), links the 'Visions' of the play's title with the series of poetic 'Visions' written by Brecht from 1938 on. See the notes to *Poems 1913–1956* (hardback edition) pp. 510–11. The drummer is Hitler, the marshal Hermann Goering, whom the Communists held responsible for the Reichstag fire of 1933.]

TWO CHARACTERS

Scene 1

SIMONE

All this being ordered hither and thither remains characteristic of the little maid-of-all-work so long as the hither and the thither are still undefined, and the hither and thither is not contrasted with something else. This would be the case were she, for instance, to be rent apart between the wishes of those above her and the needs of those below—for she is exploited from on top and from underneath—and if, to form the contrast, there were something at some particularly rending moment to be observed about TANKS that was of special worry and concern to her.

Scene 6

[*our scene* 3*b*]

THE PATRON

The *patron* can only develop into a character if he acquires an evolution of his own in this scene. His confrontation with the staff becomes manly as a result of the invasion. The invasion offers him the opportunity to score a 'victory', but he shouldn't be too eager to pick up this particular laurel wreath. It is essential that he should fall into a rage on hearing that his brickworks has been destroyed; this is not the kind of war he wants to wage. Waging it in such way destroys the point of war. Patriotic feelings raise their head later, as inhibitions. How is it going to look if he hands a French citizen over to the Germans? That would be setting a bad example.

[BBA 1190/50. For the renumbering of scenes, see the Editorial Note.]

Editorial Note

When Brecht and Feuchtwanger discussed collaborating on a play at the end of October 1942 they considered various possibilities before settling on a St Joan story:

> A confused person has dreams in which the characters of the patriotic legend take on features of her superiors, and she learns how and why those superiors are waging their war, and how long for.

Thus the note in Brecht's journal, which calls the project *Saint Joan of Vitry (The Voices)*. According to Feuchtwanger's recollection many years later the heroine was originally to be called Odette, but in what must be one of the earliest plans she is Jeanne Gotard. This was for a play of eleven scenes, starting:

1. the germans attack france. jeanne gotard is given an old book with the story of jeanne d'arc.
2. joan of arc calls on the king.
3. jeanne gotard hides the petrol stocks from the advancing german tanks.

—and finishing:

7. incendiarism of jeanne gotard.
8. respectable frenchmen talk to respectable englishmen.
9. arrest of jeanne gotard.
10. initiation of proceedings against joan of arc.
11. condemnation of jeanne gotard by a french court.

What seems like the beginning of a treatment in Brecht's typing is headed *Saint Joan of Vitry* and goes as follows:

> In Vitry, a small town in Champagne, during the German invasion of 1940, a young girl by the name of Jeanne Gotard dreamt a strange dream lasting five consecutive nights. By day she worked her father's petrol pump, he being a soldier serving in the Maginot Line. The schoolmaster across the way had lent her an old book with the illustrated story of Joan of Arc, and so at night she dreamt she was Joan. In her dreams however the historical events reported in the book were intermingled with memories of certain incidents at the petrol station, so that the

story of the saint displayed strange variations which not only
made a profound impression on those listeners to whom she
recounted her nightly experiences but would also certainly have
interested an historian, if such a person had been present. In her
dreams she appeared armed with bayonet and steel helmet, but
the rest of her clothes were those that she wore every day, while
the historical personalities with whom she had to deal—king,
marshals, cardinals and ordinary people—bore the faces of
familiar personalities of the town of Vitry, such as visited the
petrol station in the daytime. Coulonge the banker merely wore
a plumed hat, the mayor of the town simply a flowing cloak over
his grey suit . . .

A nine-scene version of the plan eliminates the missing scenes 4–6
of the scheme given above, and renames the heroine Michèle.
Thus:

1. the germans attack france. michèle gotard reads a patriotic
   legend.
2. joan of arc, summoned by divine voices, crowns the king in
   rheims and unites all frenchmen against the hereditary foe.
3. michèle saves stocks from the advancing german tanks.
4. joan of arc, rewarded by the mighty and dismissed in her
   native village, is moved by the divine voices to continue the
   struggle.
5. michèle's incendiarism.
6. highly-placed frenchmen talk to highly-placed englishmen.
7. michèle is betrayed and is arrested by the germans; however,
   certain circles arrange for her to come before a french court.
8. joan is perturbed by the angel's failure to appear, the high
   court meets and questions her about the voices.
9. condemnation of michèle gotard by a french court.

With the much more elaborately worked out plan given above on
pp. 244–8 Michèle Gotard finally became Simone Machard, but the
English decision to hand Joan of Arc over for trial by her own
people—which Feuchtwanger saw as the pivotal point of the play
—got swallowed in the next scene. None the less this eight-scene
version seems to have served as the basis for the actual writing of
the play.

Brecht's first typescript is in eight scenes, bearing the dates
28.12.42 at scene 5 and Jan 43 near the end; a note in his handwriting calls it 'first script, written in California'. An almost en-

tirely rewritten script follows, which is not in Brecht's typing and bears corrections by his and other hands; it was among his collaborator Ruth Berlau's papers and is headed 'a play in two acts by Bertolt Brecht and Lion Feuchtwanger' with three suggested English titles: *Simone Hears Voices, St Joan in Vichy* and *The Nights of St Joan*. Feuchtwanger seems to have used a copy of this, lacking Brecht's last revisions, for a third, slightly modified version which he headed 'a play in eight scenes by Bertolt Brecht and Lion Feuchtwanger' and sent to Elisabeth Hauptmann in Berlin a year before Brecht's death; it bears no marks by Brecht. The fourth and final script derives likewise from the rewritten version; it dates from 1946 and contains none of Feuchtwanger's modifications, but is heavily corrected by Brecht, who at some points went back to the first version. This is the script which was used for the German collected edition and accordingly is the basis of our own text. We shall refer to them respectively as the first version, the Berlau script, the Feuchtwanger script and the 1946 or final version.

For Brecht there were two principal points of uncertainty in the writing of it. The first was the question of Simone's age; he found himself wanting to make her younger and younger ('mainly because i cannot give a motive for her patriotism', he noted in his journal), yet by doing so he destroyed her interest as a character. 'The difficulty is', he noted on 8 December 1942 of his struggle with the 'Handshake' scene,

> i'm writing the scene with no picture of the principal part, simone. originally i saw her as a somewhat ungainly, mentally retarded and inhibited person; then it seemed more practical to use a child, so i'm left with the bare functions and nothing to offset them with in the way of individuality.

The other problem was the ending, which is unresolved in the first script and may well have been left in some confusion when Brecht went off to New York on 8 February. As will be seen from the detailed analysis that follows, he envisaged two alternative solutions, arguing (in the journal entry for 5 January) that

> the correct version is unperformable. in reality of course the wendells [i.e. the De Wendels of the Schneider arms firm] and pétains made use of the defeat and the foreign occupation to do down their social opponents. simone accordingly would need to be released by the germans (following false evidence by the staff

of the hostellerie) then handed over to the corrective institution by madame mère and captain fétain for subversive activities. in the performable version this would have to be blurred over; condemning simone for incendiarism due to her hatred of the *patron* means at the same time saving her from execution by the germans.

It was only in the final version that he seems to have settled for the less blurred alternative.

But besides these a number of other important variables can be observed in the scripts, though Brecht himself had nothing to say about them. They are:

(*a*) The identification of the angel with Simone's brother. At the beginning of the first version it is the Archangel Michael, while there is also a note saying 'the angel's voice is [? the voice] of the people'.

(*b*) The characters of Maurice and Robert, who in the first version are brothers. There they are shown shirking the call-up, and Maurice has evidently refused to help move the refugees (as is made explicit in the Berlau script). However at the end of the Berlau (ii) and Feuchtwanger scripts they turn against the *Patron*. Not so in the final script.

(*c*) The character of Père Gustave. He seems much more unpleasant in the earlier versions, bootlicking the *Patron* and giving evidence against Simone.

(*d*) The role of the mayor, who compromises at a different stage in each version. Thus in the Feuchtwanger and Berlau (ii) versions of the Fourth Dream (i.e. our scene 4a) he is still defending Simone, whereas in the final text he is one of her judges.

(*e*) The *Patron*'s journey with the two truck drivers. In our version it is not explained how they came back, nor why they brought back the china and not the wines (initially the Captain's) nor what happened to such refugees as they found room for. In the other texts the party runs into the Germans and/or breaks down, but again it is far from clear what is really supposed to have happened.

(*f*) The role of the refugees is heavily stressed in the final text, which brings in the notion of their being a 'mob' quartered in the village hall.

(*g*) Simone's escape is exclusive to the last version, though she half-tries in the Berlau and Feuchtwanger scripts.

(*b*) The placing of the Daydream varies. This was the section of the play which Feuchtwanger in a letter of 27 March 1943 told Brecht had displeased all with whom he had discussed it (William Dieterle, Hanns Eisler, Oskar Homolka and Berthold Viertel) and should therefore be cut.

Such points reflect a good deal of uncertainty in the authors' minds, and the effect is visible even in the final version, where the definition of the characters is further smudged by the occasional reallocation of lines. Besides this there is not only the altering of names—thus in the first script the mayor was Phillip [*sic*] Duclos, the *Patron* Henri Champon, his mother 'Madame Mère' and the captain Captain Bellair—but a basic insecurity about places and dates. In the earlier scripts the scope of the action embraced Saint-Nazaire, Tours and Lyons—places several hundred kilometres apart and all of them far from the Champagne country where the previous scheme of the play was laid. Again, where the final text puts Simone's village on one of the main roads from Paris to the South, the Berlau script puts it on the Paris–Bordeaux road. The cumulative effect of all these hesitations and improbabilities helps to weaken the play.

2. SCENE-BY-SCENE ACCOUNT

The following is a scene-by-scene account of the main changes. It uses the numbering of the final text with, in brackets, the numbers and titles of the corresponding eight-scene arrangement. It is followed by a short account of Feuchtwanger's novel *Simone*, which was a product of the play but, so far as we know, involved no collaboration by Brecht.

1. *The Book* (1)

The first version had Simone on stage from the start, reading her book; her present moves and business come from the Berlau script, which also changes the provenance of the book from 'the nuns' (first version) to 'the schoolmistress' and then, in Brecht's hand, to 'the *Patron*', as now. The soldier Georges's dialogue with Simone about the beauties of France was reworked more than once, and is altogether missing in the Feuchtwanger script. An addition to the Berlau script reads, in lieu of the lines from 'Is that what it says in the book?' to 'Do you have to go down to the village hall again . . .':

Simone nods

GEORGES: Perhaps they mean the cafés with their orange awnings or the *Halles* in the early morning, full of meat and vegetables.

SIMONE: What do you like best?

GEORGES: They say one's own fish, white bread and wine are best.

SIMONE: What's the most beautiful thing you've seen?

GEORGES: I don't know. In Saint-Malo, for instance, I saw the launching of the *Intrépide*, a big blue box for catching cod. We went to a bistro and drank so much *framboise* that my cousin Jean fell out of his swing-boat.

SIMONE: Was he hurt?

GEORGES: No, he fell on the fat proprietress. What do you like best?

SIMONE: When they give us milk rolls at school.

GEORGES: Yes, that's something that could stay the way it is. Same with playing bowls in the shade outside the mairie, wouldn't you say? And the women would be all right, particularly the girls in Lyons or Arles, say, pleasant ways they've got, but then you're not interested in that. Yes, there's quite a lot one could put up with.

SIMONE: And our hostellerie?

GEORGES: Just like France. Certain people spoil the whole picture so to speak.

The reference to the sappers which follows (with the mention of Simone's brother) derives from the same script, as does the dialogue between Père Gustave and the *Patron* (up to his exit on p. 8) and most of the ensuing detail about 'the gentleman with the trout' and his meal. Only part of this is in the Feuchtwanger script, while the first script goes almost straight from Georges's attempt to take away Simone's book to the sappers' actual entry on p. 8 (though it does make the point that Simone is holding down her brother's job while he is at the front). The fact that the brother is Saint-Martin's only volunteer comes from the Berlau script; the phrase 'And the people are the enemy' (p. 9) is from an addition to the 1946 version. Virtually everything from the Colonel's exit (p. 11) to the Mayor's entry (p. 12) is new in the Berlau script; in the first version the Mayor arrives before the Colonel leaves, and is bawled out for permitting the confusion on the roads; the Colonel threatening to report him to the Préfecture at Lyons.

Thereafter the first version moves straight from the Mayor's request for the lorries to his formal requisitioning of them (p. 13). It is at this point that the *Patron* states his prior obligation to the Captain and his wines, provoking the Mayor to speak of his duty to France.

> PATRON: Don't talk about France. You're just using an opportunity to score off the Captain because he cut your wife at the Préfet's ball in return for your taking Simone out of his service so she might go to school . . .

This leads quickly into the Mayor's demand for the petrol too. From there down to Maurice's statement (p. 14) that they know nothing about the petrol the first version is like a draft of the final text. Thereafter:

> MAYOR: So that's your answer? I see. Only a miracle can save France; it's rotten from top to bottom. *To Simone:* You've got a brother at the front; in the south, isn't he? Do you imagine he'll have any petrol for his tank? Jammed in the endless stream of refugees, he's no doubt waiting for a mortal attack by enemy dive-bombers. But I don't suppose you're any more likely than the others to tell me where I can get him some petrol, eh, Simone?
> *Simone stands motionless, then gives a dry sob and rushes away. Sighing, the Mayor turns and leaves.*

Neither the Berlau nor the Feuchtwanger script has any mention of the petrol in this scene or the Dream which follows. The former has the final text from the Mayor's entry to the *Patron*'s 'We must talk in private' (p. 13); whereupon the Mayor replies:

> No, Henri, we will no longer talk in private. I may be a bad mayor, I suppose, and have done wrong to shut an eye so often. But unless I can organize those twenty lorries for the refugees I don't know how I'll be able to look my son in the face when he gets back from the front. *He notices Simone.* Sending some of your food parcels to the village hall? You only filled the soldiers' dixie half full. I ought to have confiscated your stocks long ago.

> PATRON *threateningly:* Try it and see.
> MAYOR: How can the refugees get anywhere if they're robbed of their last sou all along the line?

PATRON: This is a restaurant, not a charitable institution. You can go, Simone.

Simone starts to go.

MAYOR *stops her. Calmly:* Any news from your brother?

Simone shakes her head.

MAYOR: I've not heard from my son either. *Quietly and bitterly to the others:* At this moment her brother can see the German tanks advancing towards him, Stukas above him, blocked roads behind him so that no reinforcements can get through to him; and here she is being expected to help exploit Frenchmen who are in trouble.

The *Patron* claims that this is undermining her respect for her employer, to which the Mayor replies 'I see', and so on to the end as in the final version.

First Dream of Simone Machard (2)

The Angel's opening speech in verse is in the first version, but not the brief dialogue between him and Simone which follows and identifies him with her brother André; a preliminary version of this is in the Berlau script. Simone's song, which had Saint-Nazaire in the first version, had Saint-Omer in the Berlau script and Rocamer in both the Feuchtwanger and the final scripts till Brecht restored Saint-Nazaire once again on the latter. Three of the four 'dream language' phrases on pp. 16, 18 and 21 are pen additions by Brecht to the final script, which already contained 'Okler greischt Burlapp' (p. 21). Two other nonsense remarks referred to in the stage directions were spelt out in the Berlau script; thus Simone's unintelligible reply on p. 18 is ('Allekiwist, Maurice') and Robert's remark (below) is ('Wihilirichi'). In the first version the whole scene is shorter. Thus after Simone's offer to clean Père Gustave's guns for him the *Patron* enters and Simone almost instantly beats her drum to summon the king with a version of her long speech on pp. 20–21. He thereupon enters, asks after her brother, confiscates the lorries and inquires about the petrol (which is not mentioned in the Berlau script). Why are the drivers lying, he asks.

SIMONE: They have to lie, or else they'll be called up, see? because the *Patron* will give up certifying that they're essential workers.

Then the sappers appear as on p. 21 and beat their dixies like bells, and the scene ends much as in the final text.

2. The Handshake (3)

There is some characteristic geographical confusion in the first version, where the *Patron*'s wines and china were to go to Saint-Nazaire and the refugees to Lyons (several hundred kilometres apart); then Lyons was changed to 'Vermillon', a place apparently invented by Brecht. The Mayor arrives in this version not with the town police but with the Sergeant from scene 1 and his two soldiers. Simone's ensuing explanation (to her mother and the *Patron*) is not included; it was worked out on the Berlau script. Then from where the Mayor weakens (p. 25) to the entry of Madame Soupeau everything is different, the drivers in particular being more uncooperative and the refugees not making an appearance:

MAYOR *weaker:* Monsieur Champon, I'm only doing my duty. All I asked was for you to put your lorries at my disposal.

PATRON *yells:* What do you want my lorries for?

MAYOR: I told you. I'm going to shift the refugees.

SIMONE: The old people and children anyhow, so as to clear Route 74 for the troops in Lyons to move up.

PATRON *stares at her, then to the Mayor, nastily:* Have you got the drivers? I'm told my men won't drive.

MAYOR *to the drivers:* Are you really refusing to evacuate the refugees?

SIMONE: No, they'll drive them. Maurice, Robert, will you drive?

MAURICE *ironically:* If Monsieur le Maire orders . . .

PATRON: Certain officials seem to be using this disastrous war as a pretext for laying down the law to the business community. But very well, then, I bow to force. My drivers can take the refugees to Vermillon.

MAYOR: Not to Vermillon; that would mean using Route 74. First to Saint-Nazaire.

PATRON: What can I have my lorries do in Saint-Nazaire? But very well, you're sheltering behind your orders and the army. I'm asking the army to do something for me in return: pack up my wine reserves and the china, because that must go too.

MAYOR: Why can't your men do that?

PATRON: Because my men are on strike. I'd be within my rights if I put them up against the wall for refusing to remove French property to safety in face of the enemy. But there's no discipline left.

MAYOR *to the sergeant:* Is that something you can put to your men, do you think? I've nothing against giving Monsieur Champon a hand to save his property.

MADAME MACHARD *sees that her daughter wants to say something:* Quiet, Simone.

SIMONE: But aren't the soldiers supposed to be bringing up the equipment for blowing the bridges?

MAURICE: No. [illegible]

SIMONE: To hold up the tanks till reinforcements come; you know. They ought to go right away.

SERGEANT: We'd have been there by now if we hadn't had to wait for the cookers on account of their not giving us a meal. I don't see why I should fall over myself to help this gentleman and his hotel; he's the one refused to feed us.

SIMONE: You'll get fed, won't he, Monsieur Henri? There'll be no room for provisions on the trucks if you're to be able to carry a proper number of refugees, will there, Maurice? I'll just get the key of the cellar.

MADAME MACHARD: Simone!

PATRON: What's got into you, Simone? I was amazed to see you bring in the Mayor against me. Go indoors at once and wash your neck, you shameless ungrateful creature.

MADAME MACHARD: Please excuse our daughter, Monsieur Champon; she has lost her head.

The *Patron*'s mother, here called Madame Mère, then enters and gives Simone the key, telling her to get wine for the soldiers. There is no mention of feeding the refugees or of the danger of looting, and it is the soldiers who then help themselves to the provisions. Simone returns with the bottles and persuades Maurice and Robert to load up. German planes dive, prompting the *Patron* to say that he must get away, as on p. 27, but his mother is also on stage and she replies contemptuously that she is staying:

Thanks to Simone's very sensible arrangements you will get to Saint-Nazaire as planned, and Maurice and Robert will take the china and the refugees south to Lyons. Is that right, Simone?

She proposes to give the town such food stocks as cannot be moved, saying (in a line later given to the Mayor) 'This is a time for sacrifices, Henri. It's a matter of showing good will' (p. 30). Then they all drink (p. 31) and the *Patron* makes his conciliatory

speech (p. 31). The drivers are told to load up with Monsieur
Machard, and leave. It is then the *Patron* himself who asks about
the petrol in the brickwords, saying:

> The Germans mustn't get it. Georges, Gustave, run down
> to the brickworks. Smash the pump and seal up the tank,
> right?
>
> MAYOR: Better set fire to it, Henri. There's an army order says
> all stocks of petrol have got to be burnt. The Germans must
> not find a single canful in any village.
>
> PATRON: Burn it? Rubbish. We'll need it. How are our forces
> to replenish their tanks when they attack? Simone, tell the
> Mayor that France isn't lost yet.
>
> SIMONE: That's a fact, Monsieur le Maire.
>
> MAYOR: But so many people are in the know, Simone.
>
> PATRON: No Frenchman could give away the secret. If I
> didn't realize that before I do now. Georges, Gustave, get
> moving.
>
> SIMONE *to Gustave:* I cleaned the garage out for you, Père
> Gustave.
>
> PÈRE GUSTAVE: Right. Patriotism seems to have become all
> the fashion around here.

Then the *Patron* says good bye to his mother (p. 32), and kisses
her and Simone. The radio is heard saying that the French will
counter-attack and not a foot of ground is to be given up. There
is no more reference to the petrol, and Madame says that she is
closing the hotel. Simone is not specifically dismissed, but the last
exchange between her and the Mayor is as in the final text, and
she picks up the *Patron*'s suitcases and slowly leaves with lowered
head.

The Berlau script is approximately the same as the final version
as far as the appearance of the representatives of the refugees
(p. 26). Then, from the Mayor's 'What is it?':

> ONE OF THE REFUGEES *excitedly:* Monsieur le Maire, we've
> heard the hotel is selling off its lorries. We insist you do
> something about it.
>
> WOMAN: There are sick people in the village hall. We can't
> take our children to Bordeaux on foot.

The Mayor replies 'Madame, Messieurs' etc. as in the final text,
and is answered by the Woman. Then this script cuts straight to
the long stage direction on p. 27, with the difference that the main

crowd of refugees does not appear. In the simultaneous dialogue which follows, the left-hand column is that of the final version. In the right-hand column however when Simone asks Robert and Maurice to take the refugees, Maurice refuses, saying 'I'm not a nurse' and telling Robert 'You've got no influence at the *mairie*. The Mayor and the *Patron* are birds of a feather; it's always us who pay the bill in the end . . .' The argument is interrupted by the announcement that the German tanks are nearly at Tours, causing the *Patron* to complain 'And my Sèvres and my vintage wines haven't yet been loaded'. An approximate version of the dialogue from 'SIMONE *angrily*' to 'VOICES *from outside*', then follows (in the final version it comes earlier, on p. 27), with the difference that Simone's anger is initially against Maurice for wanting to clear out and abandon the refugees. Here Madame enters and gives Simone the key (p. 29), and the ensuing dialogue down to her 'Is anybody going to load it for us?' (below) is more or less that of the final text. Thereafter:

SIMONE: Of course, Madame. Right, Maurice?

MAURICE: Go to hell. Pack china, with the Germans arriving? High time we were off.

MADAME MÈRE *sharply:* Nobody but the children seems to realize that French property cannot be allowed to fall into the hands of the Germans.

MAURICE *to Robert:* All right, we can help carry out the cases. *Exit with Robert to the store room.*

It continues approximately as in the final text from 'ONE OF THE REFUGEES' (p. 30) to the general dispersal (p. 31, bottom). Here Maurice, Robert and Georges also leave; Maurice poses the question about the brickworks as he goes, after which the dialogue is a blend of the first and final versions until the *Patron* takes his leave. Asked yet again about the petrol (this time by the Mayor) he says to ask his mother. In the Feuchtwanger script Simone then suggests getting Georges and Père Gustave and blowing it up, but in the Berlau script this is changed to a mere inquiry what should be done.

MADAME MÈRE: Didn't you hear what the *Patron* said? He asked us not to do anything precipitate. We can leave the problem of whether to destroy the petrol till the last minute. After all, it's still my son's property we're dealing with.

SIMONE: But it would be terrible if the Germans used our
    petrol to fill up, like they did in Abbeville. Wouldn't it,
    Monsieur le Maire?
MAYOR: It hasn't come to that yet by a long chalk.
The rest of the scene is virtually as in the final text.

Second Dream of Simone Machard (4)
The first version and the Berlau script both have Père Gustave in
lieu of the soldier Georges as a member of Simone's bodyguard;
neither establishes the identification of the *Patron*'s mother as
Queen Isabeau. When Simone calls on the angel (p. 36) both
versions have her sitting on the ground and beating her drum,
crying 'Come here, you Frenchmen, the enemy has arrived'. In the
Berlau script there is no reaction; she calls Georges and drums
harder, then calls on the Angel. The first version makes the Angel
St Michael. Also it has no mention of the Mayor's dream language (p. 34). The Angel's song 'After the Conqueror' (p. 36)
is slightly different in the first version, which omits the previous
recitative ('Maid, hear me' etc.) and the dialogue with Simone
after that.

3. *The Fire*
In the first version subscene (*a*) bears this title and is scene 5,
while subscene (*b*) is scene 6, The Betrayal, and is followed by the
Daydream of Simone Machard. In the Berlau and Feuchtwanger
scripts the Daydream is incorporated in the second of these two
scenes (instead of, as now, in the first).

(*a*) (5. The Fire)
At the beginning of the scene the exchange where Georges sus-
pects that Simone has been fired, the mention by Père Gustave of
the 'mob from the hall' (p. 38) and Simone's wondering if seeing
a person in a dream means that he is dead (p. 39) are none of
them in the first version, while the actual entry of the refugees
(p. 39) occurs only in the final script. Thereafter there are extensive differences. In the first script the Captain enters at this point,
saying that the Mayor will come. 'And another thing. I've been
told there were cases of looting and blackmail in these parts
yesterday. Order and discipline are herewith re-established: you
get me, my friends?' He is followed instantly by Père Gustave.
The Captain thereupon delivers a version of the speech which now
comes just before the Daydream:

CAPTAIN: Ah, Monsieur le Maire, I trust your wife is in good health. I just wanted to tell you, Duclos, that France's one hope of avoiding total disaster is to collaborate as honourably as she can with the gentlemen of the German General Staff. Paris is overrun with Communists, and here too all kinds of things occurred yesterday without the authorities lifting a finger. To put it in a nutshell, the Commandant is fully aware of this hotel's connection with a certain brickworks. You might like to take action accordingly, Duclos. Wait a moment before you follow me out, or it'll look as if I had to have you dragged down here. *Goes in.*

This is much the same in the Berlau script. Then Simone and the Mayor conduct their dialogue about the brickworks, from his (present) entry (p. 41) to his exit, which in the final version becomes '*He is about to go in*' (p. 42), allowing the Captain to re-enter with his speech roughly as above. All the present dialogue from Madame Soupeau's entry (p. 39) to the entry of the Mayor is an addition to the final script.

In the earlier versions the dialogue with Georges and Père Gustave which now follows the Daydream runs straight on from the Mayor's exit, with slight differences. Thereafter from the entry of the German soldier to the end of (*a*) everything else is the same except that the German captain (or commandant in the first version) says nothing. The Berlau script however inserts the following dialogue before 'So neither of you . . .' (p. 44):

SOLDIER [i.e. GEORGES]: What are you after? Oh, the petrol, is it? Don't you touch it. You keep out.

SIMONE: But the *Patron* said it was up to us.

SOLDIER: The *Patron*'s gone, but you're here. They'll shoot you down like a mad dog. *He draws her downstage. Urgently:* Simone, promise me you'll be sensible.

SIMONE: But you said yourself that they're bringing up whole new regiments. They broke through against the 132nd, you said.

SOLDIER: But not against the 7th [her brother's unit, in this version].

SIMONE *quietly:* That's not true, Monsieur Georges.

PÈRE GUSTAVE: Don't you get mixed up with the Germans. Sabotage can cost you your neck.

SOLDIER: It all comes from that damned book of yours. You've

been reading it all day again, then you go and imagine you're
God knows who, isn't that it?

Apart from the first sentence this is not in the Feuchtwanger
script. But from then on to the end of (a) both are practically
identical with the final text.

(b)   (6. The Betrayal)
The first version specifies that this occurs three days after (a). In
all three of the early scripts the scene starts with Georges reading
the paper as the German captain saunters across the stage and into
the hotel. Simone brings a hot-water bottle for the *Patron*'s
mother, who is unwell. Then Simone wonders about the signifi-
cance of seeing a person in a dream (the passage now near the
beginning of (a)) and her parents enter, delighted that M. Machard
has got the council job. It appears that the *Patron* has returned;
the Berlau and Feuchtwanger scripts add that he and Maurice were
held up by German tanks. In all three versions he comes in with
Robert, looking pale and sleepless. All this is prior to the beginning
of the present subscene (b), but from then on the dialogue continues much as in the final text up to where Simone says that she
will confess to the Germans to save the *Patron* (p. 47). The main
differences are (1) that the Machard parents are present up to the
firing of Georges; (2) that there is no mention of the refugees in
the village hall; (3) that in lieu of Père Gustave's remark about the
hotel's sudden popularity (p. 47) Robert tells Simone that the
Peugeot has been stolen, that one of the lorries has broken down
and that Maurice is bringing back the other. Thereafter however
the scene ends differently.

    In the first version it ends quickly, with the *Patron* assuring
Simone that since she no doubt meant well he will stand by her,
then going into the hotel without saying whether she is really
fired or not. Robert asks if he will betray her, and Georges says
'He can't do that. After all he is a Frenchman'. The Mayor and
the Captain walk across the stage into the hotel; Simone bows to the
Mayor, who pays no attention. That is the end of the scene, and the
Daydream follows.

Daydream of Simone Machard

In the first version there is no game of cards. The *Patron* is present,
and the Captain enters later, bringing the German captain as an

'unknown knight' with whom the French are invited to collaborate. He offers the Mayor a cigar, but the drumming starts again and the Mayor refuses. There are no references to 'the mob'; Madame boxes the *Patron*'s ears, not the Mayor's, and the dream ends with the German captain saying 'Of course the Maid must be got rid of'.

In the Berlau and Feuchtwanger scripts, after Simone has said that she will confess to the Germans (as above) Madame Machard reappears to say that the Mayor has given the council job to 'old Frossart' instead of to her husband, who has been 'dropped like a hot potato'. 'The Mayor', comments Georges, 'is scared of his own courage'. This leads straight into the Daydream. Mayor, captain and *Patron* sit playing cards, and neither Madame nor the German Captain appears. After 'if I am to sell my wine' (p. 43) the *Patron* says 'Have you really decided to support her, King Charles the Seventh? And given her father the council job?' The Mayor announces his determination much as in the final version, then sits down. The dream ends with the Captain pointing this out to the *Patron* and saying 'There you are, Henri; France doesn't support her any more'.

A quite different concluding section follows in both these scripts. After the dream Simone says she must leave, then Maurice arrives, having heard about the explosion:

MAURICE: Are you crazy, Simone? How could you?

SIMONE: He won't give me away.

MAURICE: Put your things on at once, you must get out of here. I'll drive you. Pack up whatever she needs most, Madame Machard.

MADAME MACHARD: I don't understand you people. You aren't expecting her to throw up her job?

GEORGES *to Maurice:* You really think he might . . .?

MAURICE *shrugs his shoulders:* If he cares about saving his wretched hotel he'll have to. They might have used the petrol as a way of showing how ready they are to collaborate. She's put a spoke in that. There's only one thing left for them to do: turn her in. *With emphasis:* At this moment she's got no more vindictive enemies in the world than Madame Mère and her respected son.

ROBERT: You're exaggerating. After all, they are French.

MAURICE: Didn't you get what they were saying on the radio?

GEORGES: Wasn't listening. What was it?

MAURICE: The Marshal has dissolved the government and taken over all its powers. That means open collaboration. Meantime *she*'s still at war.

ROBERT: The *Patron* said he'd stand by her.

MAURICE: He hadn't been told about the radio announcement. Get your things on, Simone.

SIMONE *still absent-mindedly*: I can't leave, Maurice.

GEORGES: Ten minutes back you were saying you must.

SIMONE: That was only because I was imagining things. But the *Patron* won't give me away.

MADAME MACHARD: But, Messieurs, don't give the girl crazy ideas. She can't possibly give up her job now, when the rent's due. What with our André being away as well.

PATRON *comes out of the hotel, very excited*: Simone! You've got to disappear! At once! Maurice, get her out of here! Doesn't matter where. Got that?

MAURICE: Yes sir.

PATRON: It's a matter of minutes. *Goes back into the hotel.*

ROBERT: So he *isn't* going to give you away.

MAURICE: He's given her away already. Did you see how he'd been sweating? Get a move on, Simone!

SIMONE: No, no, no. I don't want to leave. He's not going to touch me. He only came out to help me.

MAURICE: He's got a bad conscience, that's all.

Simone obstinately stays put.

GEORGES: What have you got against leaving?

SIMONE: I can't. Suppose my brother comes back. I promised him I'd be here and keep his job for him.

MAURICE: That's enough. *He seizes her, picks her up over his shoulder and carries her struggling into the garage.* Go outside the hotel, Georges, and whistle if the coast is clear. *Exit with Simone.*

Georges goes out into the road. During what follows he is heard whistling.

MADAME MACHARD: I knew it would come to this. Her brother's to blame, and all that book-reading.

SIMONE'S VOICE *from outside*: I'm not going. I can't. You don't understand.

MADAME MACHARD: What have I done to deserve it?

ROBERT: Oh, do shut up. Don't you realize that she'll be shot if they catch her?

MADAME MACHARD: Simone? Holy mother of God! *Sits distraught at the foot of the petrol pump.*
Exit Robert into the garage.
Enter from the hotel the Patron and the Captain.

PATRON: Simone! Père Gustave! *To the Captain:* Actually she was discharged some days ago. But went on hanging around my yard, so I've been told.

CAPTAIN *notices Madame Machard:* Isn't that her mother?

PATRON *embarrassed:* Ah, Madame Machard. Have you by any chance seen Simone?

MADAME MACHARD: No, Monsieur Henri, I'm looking for her myself. That girl's always doing errands for the hotel, Monsieur le Capitaine.
Père Gustave enters from the store room.

PATRON: Oh, there you are, Père Gustave. Go and get Simone, would you?
Père Gustave goes obediently up the road. The whistling stops.

PATRON *to the Captain:* I just can't imagine what put the idea in her head.

CAPTAIN: It's not as hard as all that, Monsieur Soupault. But it'll all be sorted out.

PÈRE GUSTAVE *coming back, as Georges's whistling is heard once more:* I can't find her, Monsieur Henri. Georges says she left half an hour ago.

CAPTAIN *sceptically:* Too bad that you people 'can't find her', Monsieur Soupault. *Turns and goes into the hotel.*

PATRON *mopping his perspiration:* Thank God for that.

MADAME MACHARD: In the nick of time. The things we have to go through for our children!
Maurice appears at the garage door.

PATRON: Why are you still here, Maurice? Shouldn't you be ...

MAURICE: Did she come out this way? She broke away from me.
Simone comes in from the street, with Georges behind her.

PATRON: Are you out of your mind? Quick, quick ...

SIMONE: You aren't going to give me away, are you, Monsieur Henri?

PATRON: I told you to disappear. And now—*Furious gesture of helplessness.* First you set fire to my brickworks. I don't say a word, though it's *I* who have to take the can with the Germans. And now you're being pigheaded just so as to make things harder for me. They can shoot you for all I care; I wash my hands of it.

The German captain comes out of the hotel in helmet and greatcoat, with the Captain behind him.

CAPTAIN: But we'll do everything we can, sir. Give us two hours.

Simone has instinctively tried to hide behind the Patron. He steps to one side so that she is seen.

CAPTAIN: Why, here she is. Here's our arsonist, sir.

THE GERMAN CAPTAIN: A child like that?

Pause.

PATRON: Simone, this is a pretty kettle of fish.

All this is omitted from the final version, where the dialogue about the German poster ('It all depends whether she' p. 48 to Père Gustave's 'I told you nothing of the sort' below) has been brought forward from the beginning of scene 8 in the earlier versions, and the rest is new.

4. *The Trial*
(*a*) *Fourth Dream of Simone Machard* (7)
In the first version this takes place 'during the night of 18–19 June' (i.e. three days earlier than in the final text). All three earlier scripts specify that the confused music is to 'continue the motifs of the Third Dream'. In the first version there is only one soldier with the German captain.

Down to the entry of the judges all three are more or less the same as the final text, and the first version continues so as far as the point where they put their heads together (p. 52). In the Berlau and Feuchtwanger scripts however there are at first only three judges, the Mayor suddenly appearing beside them 'in the capacity of a defence counsel'; nor does Simone identify them one by one as they come in but all at once when they uncover their faces. Otherwise these two scripts continue close to the final version down to the end of the scene, the main later additions being the reference to the refugees in the village hall and Madame Soupeau's concluding line. In the first version a number of the lines were differently allotted, though their wording remains the same: thus Père Gustave's call for accusers from the public (p. 52) and his challenge to the Angel (p. 55) were given to Simone's father, while it was the Mayor who called for a chair for Queen Isabeau and asked Simone 'Where does God dwell? . . .' (p. 54).

(*b*)   (8. The Trial)

The first version gives two alternative scenes, one of them incomplete and each differing widely from the other. The Berlau script also gives two texts, the first of which peters out in a series of shorthand notes, while the second is identical with that of the Feuchtwanger script. Altogether, therefore, there are four main variants of this scene: the first version (i) and (ii), the Feuchtwanger version (which seems to have been worked out from Berlau (i) and possibly copied in Berlau (ii)), and the final 1946 text.

In the first version (i) there is no flag visible, and the Mayor, *Patron*, his mother and the Captain are on stage at the start, as well as the four of the final version. A German soldier marches Simone in, hands the Mayor a document, salutes and leaves. The document gives the responsibility of dealing with Simone to the local authorities.

> CAPTAIN: The tone of the document is severe, but the contents are very decent. The Commandant is leaving it to the local authority to interrogate the incendiarist. Monsieur le Maire, do your duty by the commune of Saint-Martin.
>
> MAYOR *sighing:* Simone, the Germans have handed you back to your own authorities. You are strongly suspected of sabotage, a crime for which one can be shot. However the authorities have been able to raise some doubt as to the deliberateness of your intention to commit sabotage. Do you understand the purpose of this inquiry?
>
> SIMONE: Yes, Monsieur le Maire.
>
> MAYOR: Luckily the question is easily settled. Now listen carefully. If you caused the fire *before* the Germans put up their poster forbidding the destruction of essential stocks then it was not sabotage. Suppose you had done it after the poster, it would have been sabotage and we wouldn't save you. Do you understand that? Did you see the poster?

The dialogue follows as on p. 48 (which is where it was shifted to in the final text), except that there it is the *Patron*, not the Mayor who asks the questions. After Père Gustave's 'I told you nothing of the sort' (p. 48) it goes on:

> MAYOR: Père Gustave, you have offered to give evidence to the effect that Simone set fire to the brickworks. But you insist that she did it before the German order?

PÈRE GUSTAVE *avoiding Simone's eye:* Yes.

ROBERT: Oh, you've volunteered to give evidence, have you?

MADAME MÈRE: Quiet, Robert.

MAYOR: It's all perfectly clear. *To Simone:* Will you show us where the red poster was displayed? Come along, it'll still be there.

SIMONE: But I saw it before that, Monsieur le Maire.

MAYOR: Don't be difficult. This is official.

Mayor, Patron and Captain leave with Simone through the gateway.

PÈRE GUSTAVE: I had to, because of what I let out when the *Patron* drove off.

MAURICE: Shut up.

GEORGES: The Mayor's a decent man. He's whitewashing her to the Germans, and they'll let her off.

MAURICE: They're a lot of crooks. All they're doing is whitewash Saint-Martin against any suspicion that there might be Frenchmen here [cf. p. 61 in our text]. They're set on collaborating with the Germans. Simone's right. It's as though she knew what tune they were going to play.

ROBERT: We won't have heard the last of it. You wait.

Then the party returns with Simone, and the Mayor says he thinks the Germans will agree that it was not sabotage. The Captain differs, and the *Patron*'s mother says 'It was a base act of revenge against my son and myself'.

MAYOR: Revenge? What for?

MADAME MÈRE: Because we dismissed her. It's quite simple.

MAYOR: Henri, do you believe that?

PATRON *forcefully:* I refuse to stand up for this creature any longer. I offered her a chance to get away; she insisted on staying. I'm through with her. I've had enough to worry about.

Then Madame sends Maurice, Robert, Père Gustave and Georges back to their work, and they leave. She starts cross-examining Simone, approximately as from where she speaks *To Simone* (p. 58) to Simone's 'I did it because of the enemy' (p. 60). Then she tells Thérèse to 'fetch the sister' and delivers a speech that is partly the Captain's 'The least our guests can expect . . .' (p. 60) and partly her own 'The child is insubordinate' etc. (p. 62) of the final text. Thérèse returns with an Ursuline nun.

MADAME MÈRE: Sister Michèle is being so good as to take this unfortunate child into the educational establishment run by the strict sisters of St Ursula.

SIMONE *trembling:* No, no! Not to St Ursula's! I did it because of the Germans. I want to stay.

The sister takes her arm and leads her to the gateway.

SIMONE: André! André!

There it breaks off at the foot of a page.

The first version (ii), headed in Brecht's hand 'Second version, January 43', likewise breaks off at the foot of a page, this time towards the end of Madame's interrogation of Simone. It starts with Maurice, Robert, Georges and Père Gustave on stage, as in the final version, but with two German sentries. They are discussing Simone's examination by the Mayor, which has taken place offstage and in the German captain's presence, but evidently went much as in (i). Georges says 'I don't see why he doesn't do the interrogating himself, Maurice'.

MAURICE: Well, you saw how angry it made him yesterday when he heard it was a child. Shooting children doesn't go all that well with their policy of dishing out soup on the square in front of the *mairie*. The Captain had supper with him last night. I can tell you exactly how the conversation will have gone. *He mimics the German captain and the French captain in turn.* 'Bad show. I'll have to shoot her'.—'That'll put the kybosh on peaceful collaboration for the next couple of years, sir.'—'What's the answer?' 'Collaboration, my dear captain. Leave the case to us.'—'Then tomorrow pop goes the water tower, eh, Monsieur? Here's our radio announcing every hour that the French population is receiving us with open arms, wants nothing but peace.'—'My dear captain, but whoever says the person responsible was acting against the Germans?'—'Aha . . . I see. You mean you can prove that she did it *before* . . .' So that now she did it *before* the proclamation, d'you see?

Then the *Patron* enters and tells Père Gustave that his evidence won't be needed: 'A child: what do you expect?' etc. (p. 56). Georges's ensuing remarks finish with him saying that someone betrayed her.

PATRON: You dare to say that to me after I've stood here and told her she must get away?

He seizes the wounded Georges by the arm, and there is a struggle
in which Robert joins till it is interrupted by the entry of the
German captain. The captain tells the two sentries to follow him
and leaves.

> PÈRE GUSTAVE: He's taking his men away. Does that mean
> that Simone's been let free?
> MAURICE: I'd be extremely surprised.
> GEORGES: Anyhow that boche with the monocle realizes that
> Captain Bellaire isn't the only person around here. Monsieur
> le Capitaine has had his innings. They couldn't conceal the
> fact that there are still some Frenchmen in France. Ow! Even
> kids of thirteen can show them, eh, Maurice?

But the Mayor's two policemen appear at the gate, then Madame
leads in Simone from the hotel, with the Mayor and the Captain
following, and they all go into the store room. Maurice makes his
remark about whitewashing Saint-Martin, and the *Patron* angrily
orders the policemen to clear the yard.

> MAURICE: Let's go. There's nothing we can do here for the
> moment. They've got their police and they've got the Ger-
> mans. *Draws Robert and Georges away.* Poor Simone. Too many
> enemies.
> GEORGES *hoarsely:* Look out, Monsieur Henri, other times are
> coming. And when they come we'll be asking you about
> Simone. *Exeunt all three.*

The party then emerges from the store room, and Madame con-
ducts her interrogation of Simone on lines rather closer to the
final text, including a mention of 'the mob from the village hall'.
This version breaks off with Madame's 'How did you know the
Germans would discover . . .' (p. 59).

Finally the Feuchtwanger script (identical with Berlau (ii))
starts with much the same stage direction as our text, but without
Georges and with the addition of the two German sentries. It
opens with Maurice's remark about the Marshal; Simone however
has not got away but is being interrogated as in the first version
(ii). Georges, who has been giving evidence, comes out of the
hotel to report that they are all behaving very decently, even
Madame and the Captain. The German captain has said 'that these
are tragic days and he has no desire to hurt Frenchmen's feelings'.
He is allowing the others to establish Simone's ignorance of the
poster because, as Maurice puts it, 'I don't imagine they want to

start off their armistice and their formal collaboration by shooting our children'.

GEORGES *scratching his head:* Do you think nothing's going to happen to her?

MAURICE: That's another question.

ROBERT: If they do anything to Simone I'm coming to Algiers with you, Maurice. *To Georges:* The radio says the old government's going to carry on the fight from there.

GEORGES *moving his arm thoughtfully:* That's what one ought to do.

PÈRE GUSTAVE: They talk a lot on the radio.

Then the *Patron* enters as in the first version (ii), leading on to the struggle and a version of the ensuing dialogue as far as Madame Soupeau's entry with Simone (but no policemen) and disappearance into the store room.

PATRON *complainingly, as he dusts down his suit:* I gave her an opportunity to disappear. She insisted on staying. She's caused me nothing but trouble from the very first. A hundred thousand francs, she's cost me. As for the cost to my nerves, I can't count it. And now she's causing bad blood between me and my old employees. That's what comes of trying to protect her. Well, the time for sentimentality is over. I shan't interfere any more. Not that I bear you people a grudge. She upset all of us. Back to work, Maurice and Robert!

Maurice and Robert stay put.

PATRON: Didn't you hear me?

MAURICE: Robert and I will just wait and see what's happening to Simone.

The party leaves the store room, and this time Madame's interrogation of Simone is witnessed and occasionally interrupted by Robert, Maurice and Georges. It is longer than in the final version, though largely coinciding with it, and ends with an admission by Simone that she was acting on her own, not on the Mayor's orders.

MADAME SOUPEAU: To settle a score with the hotel.

PATRON: And to think Maman told lies to the Germans to make them set you free!

The two policemen enter, and thereafter the script stays close to the final text, except that there are no nuns and the institution is the 'House of Correction at Tours'; (an addition to the Berlau (ii) script in Brecht's hand introduced the 'brutal looking lady' and the comments indicating that this was a place for the mentally handicapped). However, instead of fetching her things from the store room, as in the final text, she says good-bye to Georges, Maurice and Robert until she is dragged off calling 'André! André!' There is no appearance of the Angel, and after the *Patron*'s order to resume work the ending is different.

> MAURICE: What, us? You'll find it difficult to get anyone in Saint-Martin to work for you after this. Come on.
> *Maurice, Robert and Georges turn to leave.*
> PATRON *running after them:* But Maurice! I haven't done anything to you, have I?—Five years we've been together—It was for the hotel's sake—It was for the sake of your jobs, for that matter—Maurice! Robert!
> GEORGES *at the gateway, turns round, hoarsely:* You look out. Other times are coming. When they come we'll be asking you about Simone. *Curtain.*

In the 1946 script, which our text follows, the date is given as 'Morning of June 19th'. The Mayor's order to M. Machard to clear the village hall is a typed addition. The nuns are mainly handwritten amendments (as in Berlau (ii)); the 'brutal-looking lady' remains in one stage direction (the published text makes her plural) but elsewhere is amended to 'the nuns' or 'one of the nuns'. The House of Correction is struck out, together with all references but one to Tours (the Mayor offers to give evidence there). References to St Ursula come from the first version, those to the mentally handicapped from the additions to the Berlau script, reinforced by Simone's new comment 'They chain them up!' (p. 62).

3. FEUCHTWANGER'S NOVEL

Simone, a novel by Lion Feuchtwanger, was published in 1944 by the Viking Press in a translation by G. A. Herrmann. It is less 'the book of the play' than an independent reworking of the ideas discussed in the course of the author's collaboration with Brecht, and it differs in various important respects. Thus out of twenty-one chapters only two contain Visions (as against the much more even alternation in the play) though there are three others where Simone is shown reading the books (plural) which she has been given by an old bookbinder friend. The town where the story is set is a fair-sized place, a Burgundian *chef-lieu d'arrondissement* (i.e. of the importance, say, of Châlons-sur-Saône) where the step-uncle who corresponds to the *Patron* runs a largish transport business, not a hotel. The refugees are in the Palais de Justice; the sous-préfet corresponds to the Mayor, and the local Marquis de Saint-Brisson to the Captain who wants his wines evacuated. Simone Planchard is 'a tall, lanky fifteen-year-old':

> Her bony, tanned face framed with dark blond [*sic*] hair was tense; her dark, deep-set eyes under a low but broad and well-shaped forehead eagerly absorbed all that moved before her. . . . She could scarcely be called beautiful, but her intelligent, thoughtful, somewhat stubborn face with its strong chin and prominent Burgundian nose was good to look at.

Moreover her father had been a local left-wing hero who had died in the Congo two years previously while investigating native working conditions. Madame, who corresponds to the *Patron*'s mother (and like her appears as Queen Isabeau) was evidently the father's step-mother. Thanks to her, Simone's role in the household (the Villa Monrepos) is that of an unpaid servant.

This Simone has no brother. She has a confidant in the secretary of the sous-préfecture and two friends of her own age—her schoolmate Henriette and Henriette's brother Étienne—though neither figures very largely in the story. Of her uncle's employees in the loading yard Maurice (there is no Robert, and Georges is a nonentity) is at first cruelly and gratuitously offensive to her; it looks as if he is meant to stand for the French Communists, sceptical of the bourgeoisie and their war, and uninvolved until after the German victory. In the dream episodes he figures as the monstrous Gilles de Rais. From the first Simone seems attracted to him, and once she has set fire to the yard (lorries, petrol and all) —which occurs about half-way through the book, as against two-thirds of the way through the play—he starts behaving more amicably, though still in a rather condescending way. He offers to get her away on his motor-cycle; but by the time she decides to accept his offer it is too late and he has already gone. She escapes by herself, but is arrested in Nevers and brought back.

Though Madame and the other villains (such as the lawyer Maître Levautour) seem heavily caricatured, the step-uncle's actions are generally credible and within the bounds of reason. For much of the story he even behaves kindly. 'Don't you understand', he asks her, 'that I can't live without my business? I am a business man. I can't help that'. And again, in explanation of his actions, 'Some people are born to be artists, others to be engineers; I was born to be a business man, a promoter.' To save his business and at the same time prevent the Germans from punishing the entire town he arranges with the French authorities that Simone shall confess to having caused the fire for personal reasons. This she formally does on the understanding that no proceedings will be taken against her. However, the Marquis and Madame see to it that she is sent away to the Grey House, the reformatory at 'Francheville', the departmental capital, and 'an uncouth woman' escorts her away. As she is driven off the crowd in the street makes signs to her—

> Arms were raised waving to her, women and girls wept, the gendarme had come to attention, shouts sounded in her direction: 'Good-bye, Simone—good-bye, Simone Planchard—take care of yourself, Simone—so long, Simone—we won't forget you, Simone Planchard—we'll come and get you, Simone.'

And she rides away confident 'that she would survive the Grey House'.

Notes and Variants
to *Schweyk in the Second World War*

SCHWEYK IN THE SECOND WORLD WAR

Texts by Brecht

THE STORY

The Good Soldier Schweyk, after surviving the First World War, is still alive. Our story shows his successful efforts to survive the Second as well. The new rulers have even more grandiose and all-embracing plans than the old, which makes it even harder for today's Little Man to remain more or less alive.

The play begins with a

Prologue in the Higher Regions

wherein a preternaturally large Hitler with a preternaturally large voice talks to his preternaturally large police chief Himmler about the putative loyalty, reliability, self-denial, enthusiasm, geopolitical consciousness and so on and so forth of the European 'Little Man'. The reason why he is demanding such virtues of the Little Man is that he has made up his mind to conquer the world. His police chief assures him that the European Little Man bears him the same love as he does the Little Man in Germany. The Gestapo will see to that. The Führer has nothing to fear, and need have no hesitation about conquering the world.

I

There has been an attempt on Hitler's life. Hearty applause from the 'Chalice' in Prague, where the good dog-dealer

Josef Schweyk and his friend Baloun are sitting over their morning drinks and discussing politics with the Chalice's landlady, the young widow Anna Kopecka. Fat Baloun, whose exceptional appetite presents him with special problems in these days of Nazi rationing, quickly lapses into his normal gloom. He has learnt from reliable sources that the German field kitchens will dish out sizeable helpings of meat. How much longer is he going to be able to hold out against the temptation simply to go and join up in the German army? Mrs Kopecka and Schweyk are greatly disturbed by his situation. A soul in torment! Schweyk, ever the realist, suggests making Baloun swear an oath never under any circumstances to have anything to do with the Germans. Baloun reminds them that it is six months since he last had a square meal. In exchange for a square meal, he says, he would be prepared to do *anything*. Mrs Kopecka thinks something might be arranged. She is a blazing patriot, and the idea of Baloun in the German army is more than she can bear. When her young admirer turns up, the butcher's son Prochazka, they hold a touching conversation in which she poses Cleopatra's age-old question: 'If it truly is love, then tell me how much?' She wants to know if, for instance, his love would run to the scrounging of two pounds of pickled pork for the undernourished Baloun. He could take it from the paternal shop, only the Nazis have established heavy penalties for black-marketeering. None the less, seeing the way to the widow's heart open before him for the first time, young Prochazka agrees in a positive tornado of emotion to bring round the meat. Meanwhile the Chalice has been filling up and Schweyk has started letting all and sundry know what he thinks of the Munich plot against Hitler. Inspired by the announcements on the German radio, he plunges with foolhardy innocence into a mortally dangerous conversation with Brettschneider, who is known to all the regular customers as a Gestapo agent. His classic drivelling fails to deceive the Gestapo man. Without any more ado Herr Brettschneider arrests the amazed but obliging Schweyk.

2

Introduced to Gestapo headquarters in Petschek's Bank by
Herr Brettschneider, Schweyk flings up his right hand,
bawls out 'Long live our Führer Adolf Hitler! We are going
to win this war!', and is discharged as chronically half-witted.

Hearing that Schweyk is a dog dealer, the interrogating SS
officer Ludwig Bullinger asks about a pedigree dog he has
seen in the Salmgasse. 'Beg to report, sir, I know that animal
professionally', says Schweyk cheerfully, and goes on to
expatiate on the racial question. That pomeranian is the apple
of Privy Councillor Vojta's eye, and not to be had for love
or money. Schweyk and the SS officer discuss how best to
have the Privy Councillor arrested and expropriated as an
enemy of the state; however, it turns out that he is 'no yid'
but a quisling. So Schweyk gets the honourable job of stealing
the pedigree pom and showing himself to be a good collaborationist.

3

Returning in triumph to the Chalice, Schweyk finds that a
tense situation has developed. Fat Baloun is waiting for his
meal like a cat on hot bricks, fully prepared at the first
glimpse of the meat to abjure all intention of ever joining
Hitler's army. It is now ten past twelve, and young Prochazka has not yet shown up. Schweyk has been considerate
enough to bring along SS-Man Müller II from Gestapo HQ,
with the promise that widow Kopecka will tell his future by
reading his hand. At first the landlady refuses on the grounds
that she has had unfortunate experiences with her predictions.
Young Prochazka now finally appears, and everyone looks
nervously at his music case—he is a student at the music
academy—because of course the SS-Man must not see the
meat. To get him out of the way Mrs Kopecka sits down and
reads his hand. It seems that he is destined to perform heroic

deeds, and has been picked out finally for a hero's death. Depressed and demoralized, the SS-Man lurches out and Baloun flings himself on the music case round which he has been longingly circling for some time. The case is empty. Young Prochazka makes his miserable confession: he didn't dare steal the meat because the sight of Schweyk's arrest gave him such a fear of the Gestapo. Angrily the widow Kopecka spurns him with a biblical gesture, for he has failed the test as a man and as a Czech. Despondently he leaves, but no sooner does the bitterly frustrated fat man speak slightingly of her suitor than she snaps back that the Nazis are to blame for it all. So Baloun's wrath is diverted to the oppressors of his once beautiful country, and when Herr Brettschneider the Gestapo agent comes in he starts singing the subversive song of the black radish, which must 'get out', and be 'sliced and salted' till 'he sweats', all of which strikes Herr Brettschneider as suspicious but without offering him any pretext to intervene.

First Schweyk Finale
Interlude in the Upper Regions

The mighty Hitler, having encountered obstacles in his attempt to conquer the world, needs more planes, tanks and guns, and inquires of the mighty Goering whether the European Little Man is prepared to work for him. Goering assures him that the European Little Man will work for him just like the Little Man in Germany. The Gestapo will see to that. The Führer has nothing to fear and need have no hesitation about carrying on conquering the world.

4

Schweyk's operation against the germanophil Privy Councillor Vojta's pom takes place in the gardens along the Vltava or Moldau, which is where Vojta's maidservant and her friend

Paula are accustomed to take the pedigree hound for his walkies every evening. Schweyk and Baloun come up to the bench where the two girls are sitting, and pretend to have erotic aims in view. Schweyk warns the girls in all honesty that SS-leader Bullinger wants to annex the pom for the sake of its racial purity and have it sent to his lady wife in Cologne; he has had this on impeccable authority. Thereupon he goes off 'to meet someone at the Metropole'. Baloun exchanges pleasantries with the girls, and they are moved by the Moldau's majestic flow to start singing a folk song. By the end of the song the dog has gone. Schweyk has under-handedly lured it away as they were singing. The girls rush off to the police station, and Schweyk has just returned with the pom to tell his friend that they mustn't let the SS-leader have it till he has put down the money, when a fishy-looking individual appears on the scene. Schweyk the dog-catcher has a man-catcher on his track; the individual identifies himself as a functionary of the Nazi Labour Organization whose job it is to recruit idlers and loafers into the 'voluntary labour service'. Concerned for the pom, Schweyk and Baloun are led off for registration.

5

Dinner break in the Prague goods sidings. Schweyk and Baloun have become shunters for Hitler and are waiting under the eyes of a heavily-armed German soldier for their cabbage soup to be sent up from the Chalice. Today it is widow Kopecka in person who brings their enamel dishes. The stolen pom left in her care by Schweyk is becoming the focus of some intense political activity, and must be got off the premises. The controlled press is saying that the dog's dis-appearance is due to an act of vengeance by the population against a pro-German official. Schweyk promises to come and collect it. He is only half concentrating, since he is troubled by the state of Baloun. The sentry's dinner has arrived—

goulash! Trembling from head to foot, Baloun has gone
sniffing after the pot as it was borne past him. Now he is
excitedly asking the sentry whether the helpings in the
German army are always as big as that, etc., etc., and scarcely
pays attention to the imploring glances of his friends. The
soldier is plunged in thought as he munches his goulash,
all the while silently moving his lips between gobbets. He has
been told to memorize the number 4268, being that of a
waggon with agricultural machinery for Lower Bavaria, and
this is something he finds difficult. Always ready to help,
Schweyk sets out to teach him a mnemonic technique which
he learned from a water-board statistician who was one of the
regulars at the Chalice. By the time he has finished explaining
it the poor sentry's brain is in such a tangle that when they
eventually ask him for the number he helplessly points to
any old waggon. Schweyk is afraid that this may mean that a
waggonload of machine guns for Stalingrad may get sent to
Bavaria in lieu. 'But who can tell?', he remarks consolingly
to Baloun and Mrs Kopecka. 'By that time perhaps what
they'll need most in Stalingrad will be combine-harvesters
and it'll be Bavaria's turn to want machine-guns.'

6

Saturday evening at the Chalice. Dance. A morose Baloun
takes the floor with the Privy Councillor's maidservant, who
is there with her friend. The police are still interviewing the
two girls about the pom. Yesterday however they dropped a
hint to Herr Brettschneider as to its whereabouts: at SS-
leader Bullinger's; possibly by now in Cologne. Baloun hints
that this may be his last evening at the Chalice: he is fed up
with feeling hungry. And it incidentally emerges that the
noisy fun of the dance floor serves a higher purpose: covering
up the sound of the news from London, which Kopecka is
listening to and passing on to the guests. Enter then Schweyk,
cheerfully, with a parcel under his arm: meat for Baloun's

goulash. The fat man can hardly believe it; the two friends embrace most movingly. Baloun's enthusiasm is such however that Schweyk asks Mrs Kopecka to put extra paprika in the goulash, since it's only horsemeat. The landlady looks quizzically at him, and he confesses that it is Mr Vojta's pom. A police car draws up. SS-leader Bullinger enters the Chalice, with SS-men at his heels. Hue and cry for the Vojta pom. Asked by Bullinger whether he knows the dog's whereabouts, Schweyk innocently replies that he hasn't got it. 'Didn't you see in the papers, Herr SS-leader, where it said it had been stolen?' Bullinger's patience gives way. He bellows that the Chalice is the source of all subversive Czechish subversiveness and will have to be smoked out. Moreover the dog can only be there. The SS is starting to search the place when Herr Brettschneider arrives. Herr Brettschneider, who has long pictured himself in the role of protector (this is, after all, a Protectorate) to the charming Mrs Kopecka, forcefully stands up to the fuming Bullinger and invites him to Gestapo HQ, where he has some rather revealing information about the present location of the missing dog. Mrs Kopecka's house is above suspicion; he would go to the stake for that. Unfortunately at this very moment the gentlemen's attention is drawn to a parcel reposing on one of the tables. The wretched Baloun has been unable to keep his fingers off Schweyk's gift. A triumphant Bullinger discloses the contents of the parcel: meat. So the Chalice is a centre of the black market! At that Schweyk feels forced to admit that he put the parcel there. He claims that a gentleman with a black beard gave it to him 'to look after'. All those present affirm having seen the man, while Herr Brettschneider, after going to the stake on the Chalice's behalf, thinks it very possible that the criminal spotted the SS a hundred yards off and accordingly ran away. None the less Bullinger insists on arresting Schweyk, and the gentlemen escort him out of the Chalice— Bullinger, with the parcel under his arm, prophesying that he will find that dog yet. Cold-shouldered by the widow, young Prochazka has spent the entire evening sitting in a corner;

now he slinks guiltily out, followed by the widow's icy stare. Baloun bursts into tears. Thanks to his weakness the loving couple has been parted and his friend landed in mortal danger. The Chalice's landlady consoles him. In a big song she foretells that just as the Moldau washes away all the dirt, so her oppressed people's love of their country will wash away the cruelties of their invaders.

Second Schweyk Finale
Interlude in the Upper Regions

The anxious Hitler, having been caught by the Russian winter, needs more soldiers. He inquires of the anxious Goebbels whether the European Little Man is prepared to fight for him. Goebbels assures him that the European Little Man will fight for him just like the Little Man in Germany. The Gestapo will see to that.

7

As a result of disagreements between Bullinger the crocodile and Brettschneider the tiger, and what with Hitler's screaming for fresh soldiers, the good soldier Schweyk has moved from the cellars of the Gestapo to the German Army recruiting bureau. Among those whom he encounters there is Privy Councillor Vojta, who is being sent to the front because his pom was stolen. All the inmates are discussing what loathsome diseases they can report to the doctors at their medical inspection. Schweyk for his part feels another bout of rheumatism coming, since he has no time to travel to Russia for Hitler when 'nothing's been settled in Prague'. Hearing that young Prochazka is standing outside the barracks with an important message for him, he fears the worst. Happily Prochazka manages to bribe an SS-man to smuggle in a note to him, and it is an encouraging one. The Chalice landlady's suitor writes that, having been deeply moved by Schweyk's self-sacrifice and ghastly fate, he will now supply 'the desired article'. At that Schweyk feels prepared to devote himself with an untroubled mind to Hitler's Russian affairs, said to be going none too well. Outside is heard the Nazis' notorious Horst Wessel song; a battalion is moving off to the East. The inmates begin singing their own version of the Nazi anthem, where 'The butcher calls' and they 'march like sheep'; and an NCO comes in who is mistaken enough to praise them for joining in so cheerfully, then informs them that they are all undoubtedly fit to enlist and are accordingly accepted into the army. They are to be divided among different units to prevent them from getting up to any filthy tricks, so Schweyk bids a touching farewell to the Privy Councillor and goes off to Hitler's war.

8*

Weeks have elapsed. Deep in the wintry plains of the Russian empire Hitler's good soldier Schweyk is marching to join his unit near Stalingrad, where it is supposed to combine with other sections of the Nazi army in holding back the Red Army's terrible assaults. As a result of one of his numerous misadventures he has lost contact with the rest of his draft. Untroubled by geographical preconceptions, however, and in his usual blithely trusting frame of mind, he is marching towards his allotted destination wrapped in a great bundle of assorted articles of clothing to keep out the cold. A semi-demolished signpost says that Stalingrad is 100 miles off.

While he is thus marching to Stalingrad the Chalice keeps looming up in a rosy light before our good Schweyk's eyes. He pictures to himself how young Prochazka lives up to his promises. The man's love of the landlady has overcome his fear of the Gestapo, and to her agreeable surprise he hands Mrs Kopecka two pounds of pickled pork for Schweyk's unfortunate friend Baloun.

* The stage is divided in two.

As he battles courageously against the icy blasts of the steppes the indefatigable and utterly well-intentioned Schweyk becomes uncomfortably aware that he is getting no closer to his goal. The further he marches, the greater the distances shown on the signposts to Stalingrad, where Hitler so urgently needs him. A thousand miles away Anna Kopecka may at this moment be singing her 'Song of the Chalice', that homely and hospitable place. The voracious Baloun's long-awaited meal will have developed into a wedding feast for the landlady and young Prochazka.

Schweyk marches on. The blizzards on those interminable eastern steppes, where the distance to Stalingrad always remains about the same, cloak the sun by day and the moon by night from the view of the good soldier Schweyk, who set out to give the great Hitler a helping hand.

Epilogue

It is likewise deep in the eastern steppes that the good soldier Schweyk personally encounters his Führer Hitler. Their conversation in the driving snow is brief and almost entirely swallowed by the storm. The gist of this historic conversation is that Hitler is asking Schweyk whether he knows the way back.

> [GW *Schriften zum Theater* 3, pp. 1186–96. Dated New City, May 1943. This preliminary summary of the story was made for Kurt Weill, and it contains some differences from the final text. Thus the interludes balance more neatly; there is no interlude after scene 2; and Goebbels appears instead of von Bock. This is the only version which makes Prochazka a music student (scene 3) and has Schweyk preparing for an attack of rheumatism (scene 7). It omits the Chaplain and the singing of the 'German Miserere', and the ending is unlike that of any of the scripts.]

STAGING

The Chalice bar in Prague forms the centre of the set. Black oak panelling, bar with brass fitting, electric piano with a transparent top in which the moon and the flowing Moldau can appear. In the third act only a part of the Chalice appears to Schweyk in his thoughts and dream: his own table. Schweyk's 'Anabasis' shown in this act; move in a circle around this part of the Chalice. The length of his march can be indicated by such devices as having the peasants' hut roll forwards or backwards, growing larger or smaller in the process.—The interludes should be played in the style of a grisly fairy tale. The whole Nazi hierarchy (Hitler, Goering, Goebbels) can appear in all of them (plus Himmler and von Bock as the case may be). The satraps can accentuate the verses with shouts of 'Heil!'

[Note 'Zur Inszenierung' appended to the text of the play in GW5, p. 1995.]

Editorial Note

Brecht's Schweik play derives from Jaroslav Hašek's novel *The Adventures of the Good Soldier Švejk* [or Schweik] *in the World War*, or more precisely from its German translation by Grete Reiner, which was first published in 1926 and from then on remained one of Brecht's favourite books. It was promptly dramatized by Max Brod, the Prague German writer who was responsible also for the publication of Kafka's posthumous novels, and by the German humorist Hans Reimann. The resulting play was one of those chosen by Erwin Piscator for his first season with his own company in Berlin in 1927–8, when Brecht was one of his team of dramaturgs, and because it seemed far too conventional and static for the form of production which Piscator had in mind, which was to make use of a treadmill stage and George Grosz projections, it was radically overhauled by this team. In Brecht's own mind he himself was the main author of the Piscator version of this play; thus according to *The Messingkauf Dialogues* 'he did Schweik for him entirely'. However all other accounts give Piscator's principal dramaturg Felix Gasbarra (whom Brecht did not like) an equal or even greater share in the new adaptation, and there is nothing in Brecht's papers to bear him out, beyond his pencilled title-page to the script: 'Adventures of the Good Soldier Schweik. / Brecht, Gasbarra, Piscator, G. Grosz.' Nor, so far as we know, did either he or his editors ever contemplate publishing it among his own works, even though these contain a number of adaptations, in several of which he had collaborators. It first appeared in 1974, in Herbert Knust's *Materialien zu Bertolt Brechts 'Schweyk im zweiten Weltkrieg'* (Suhrkamp-Verlag, Frankfurt), which gives a much fuller account of the play's evolution than we can do here.

Brecht's copy was probably sent him from Russia by Piscator in the early 1930s—Knust points out that it is on Russian paper—when there was some question of the two men collaborating on a script for Mezhrabpom-Film. It differs from the Brod–Reimann version above all in its attempt to match the 'epic' and picaresque form of Hašek's unfinished masterpiece. In his journal Brecht termed it a 'pure montage from the novel', though in fact it incorporated some of the earlier version and was performed under the original adaptors' names (since they held the rights and were prepared to accept this arrangement). Briefly, its first part, corresponding to the novel's part I, is divided into the following short scenes (the numbers of the relevant chapters in the book being given in brackets): 1. [1] At Schweik's. / 2. [1] At the Chalice. / 3. [7] At Schweik's (where he determines to volunteer). / 4. [7] Street scene (with Schweik in the wheelchair shouting 'To Belgrade!'). / 5. [8] Recruiting office (medical inspection). / 6. [8] Military hospital. / 7. [8] Streets in Prague (with Schweik under arrest). / 8. [9] Transformation scene: detention room, chapel, and sacristy. / 9. [14] Lieutenant Lukaš's rooms (Katz, the chaplain, loses his batman at cards). / 10. [14] The same (where Schweik fulfils the lady's wishes). / 11. [14] The same (preparatory to the stealing of the dog). / 12. Street in Prague (Schweik and sapper Voditchka as dog thieves). / 13. [3 of part II] The same (Voditchka making anti-Hungarian gestures). / 14. [15] Barrack square (the colonel recognizes his dog and packs Schweik and Lukaš off to the front).

The second part, drawn from parts II and III of the novel, is in a slightly confused order (e.g. the numbering of the second scene) and differs from the staged version in its ending. (Piscator himself recounts that his team suggested various alternatives, but that he finally settled for Gasbarra's idea, based on Cadet Biegler's dream in the original, of a scene in heaven with Schweik and war wounded parading before God; when this proved under-rehearsed however it was changed for the parting scene between Schweik and Voditchka, who agree to meet 'at six o'clock after the war'.) Again, the scenes are as follows: 1. [II/1] Transformation scene: in the train, changing to the station police office at Tábor. / 5. [II/2] Film, with Schweik marching (the start of Schweik's 'Anabasis') and episode with the herdsman. / 2. [II/2] Transformation scene: country road, then Putim police station, then film. / 3a. In a troop train (about Baloun and his hunger). / 3b. Schweik rejoins his unit. / 3c. [III/2] In the train (where Baloun has eaten the sardines). / 3d. [III/3] Beside the railway track (with Baloun doing physical jerks). / 3e. [III/2] Other side of the train (with Schweik made to do the same). Schweik here tells the 4268 episode as a story. / 4. [III/4] Battlefield. (He gets lost, puts on Russian uniform and is taken prisoner by a Hungarian unit of his own army. A shell bursts, and he is killed.) Though the typescript finished here, Knust's *Materialien* volume follows this with the closing scene which Brod wrote for Piscator after discussion with him and the dramaturgs. Called 'Schweik in Heaven, An

Epilogue', it consists of two parts, the first of which shows the entrance gate guarded by an angelic sentry, with a crowd of mutilated soldiers of all nations trying to get in. Among them are Schweik and Marek, who get through only by jumping on to the back of a general's staff car. Part 2 then shows them being marched before the Supreme Commander, who finally accepts Marek as 'a good honest atheist' but rejects Schweik on the grounds that 'the fellow will simply put a spanner in any works'. He is packed off back to earth, where he arrives just in time to keep his rendez-vous with Voditchka in the Chalice.

In returning to this material with a view to reworking it for the Second World War, Brecht found little that he could incor-porate as it stood. Discussing his plan with his son on his return from New York at the end of May 1943 he realized that he was changing Schweik's character by allowing him to risk frequenting so dangerous a pub as the Chalice (which figures little in the book), and sacrifice himself for the sake of Baloun. 'That indeed is where the situation is sharper than in 1914', he noted in his journal for 27 May, where he reports that he had been re-reading the novel in the train on the way back:

> once again i was overwhelmed by hašek's vast panorama and the authentically un-positive point of view which it attributes to the people, they being themselves the one positive element and accordingly incapable of reacting 'positively' to anything else. whatever happens schweik mustn't turn into a cunning underhanded saboteur. he is merely an opportunist exploiting the tiny openings left him.

He had already written the 'Story' for Kurt Weill before leaving New York, and it seems that he soon showed this to Eisler, who commented that Schweik could not be seen as a typical 'little man' and suggested that Brecht's play ought to end with him leading Hitler to Stalingrad, not back home. Another diary entry, of the 29th, shows that he also discussed it with Peter Lorre, whom he evidently had in mind for the title part, while again on 12 July when the first rough version was already complete, he noted that

> the language of the play differs substantially from that of the german hašek translation. south german elements have been worked in, and in various ways the gest is different. so it would be wrong, e.g., to speak bohemian dialect in this play; in other words the tone of voice shouldn't be bohemian-german.

Scene 2 of the first part of the Piscator adaptation is the only one to have survived in recognizable form, and even there Brecht changed the sex of the landlord Palivec, turning him (doubtless for Lotte Lenya's sake) first into Mrs Natonek, then changing her name to Kopecka. Most of Hašek's characters, too, he abandoned, so that aside from a brief glimpse of Father Lacina (the less interesting of Hašek's two disgraceful chaplains) only Baloun and the police agent Brettschneider appear with Schweik in the play; all other characters are Brecht's or belong to history. But the basic concept and a number of subsidiary situations or elements were transplanted into the new terms: the stealing of the dog for instance, Baloun's embarrassing appetite, the incident of waggon 4268, the notion of an 'Anabasis' with its semi-conscious loss of orientation, and above all the whole Schweikian approach to authority, patriotism and war. Though the songs were mainly Brecht's, three of Schweik's chants are taken from the book— 'He stood beside his gun' (p. 119) from II/2; 'When we marched off to Jaromiř' (p. 124) from III/4 (Piscator II/5); and 'When Hitler sent for me' (p. 126) from I/8 (Piscator I/7)—while Baloun's 'Beseda' song (p. 107) can be found in III/4, where it is described as 'the song the Czech regiments sang when they marched and bled for Austria at Solferino'. And despite what Brecht says, Schweik's whole way of speaking derives from the novel. If at times it resembles that of Mother Courage, or Matti (in *Puntila*), or even Galy Gay (in *Mann ist Mann*: another part which Brecht identified with Lorre), this is only because they too in some measure reflect the same source.

The new play was at first simply called *Schweyk*, the phrase 'in the Second World War' making its appearance as an addition on the title-page of what seems to be the latest of the four versions in the Brecht Archive. The other three of these all date from 1943 and consist of a bound copy in Brecht's typing, dated Santa Monica, July 1943; a largely identical Brecht typescript (but divided into acts and with a different ending) which he gave to Peter Lorre; and a fair copy not typed by Brecht. In summarizing their slight differences scene by scene we will refer to them respectively as the bound script, the Lorre script, the fair copy and the old Berliner Ensemble script (it bears that company's stamp). The first printed text appeared in volume X of the collected *Stücke* (1958), though a duplicated stage script was available from Henschel-Verlag in East Berlin in 1956.

2. SCENE-BY-SCENE ACCOUNT

Prologue in the Higher Regions. Our text is identical with the bound
script. The fair copy has a different version of the first three
lines:

HITLER

My dear Himmler, forty-eight is the age I've now got to.
And so henceforward 'now or never' must be my motto.
Accordingly I've just decided ['to bid for world domination',
etc.].

This version ends, after 'how does the Little Man view me?':

HIMMLER

My Führer, he loves you—at any rate that's the plan—much
as the Little Man in Germany loves you too. The Gestapo
arrange all that.

HITLER

It's just as well they do.

—thus matching the last lines of the subsequent Interlude between scenes 3 and 4, and between scenes 6 and 7.

Scene 1. Virtually unchanged from the bound script.

Scene 2. Virtually unchanged. The report about the banker
Kruscha and Bullinger's reaction to it were additions to the
first script.

Interlude in the Lower Regions. Is in the bound script but not in the
Lorre script, the fair copy, the old Berliner Ensemble script or
the duplicated stage script.

Scene 3. The fat woman is an addition by Brecht on the bound
script, which remained virtually unchanged.

Interlude in the Higher Regions. Unchanged. In the Lorre script this
begins Act 2.

Scene 4. One or two cuts have been made since the bound script,
notably a characteristic Schweyk story following after 'Yes,
the Moldau' on p. 99. The *Moritat* 'Heinrich schlief bei
seiner Neuvermählten', unattributed by Brecht, who gives it as
an appendix in the printed version, is by J. F. A. Kazner (1779);
according to Dr Sammy McLean it is also known as 'Heinrich
und Wilhelmine', 'Die Geisterstimme von Mitternacht', and

'Der ungetreue Liebhaber'. Eisler set it to the tune of a south German folksong.

In the bound script this scene was originally followed by a second 'Interlude in the Lower Regions', which Brecht cut.

Scene 5. A speech by Schweyk about sabotage, added as an afterthought to the bound script, was dropped in the fair copy.

Scene 6. All through this scene the references were to the London, not the Moscow Radio. The amendment was made on the bound script, but not on the other three, nor on the duplicated stage script. Kati's remark about Schweyk's hat (p. 114) was an addition to the bound script, which also lacks the Song of the Moldau at the end, presumably because Brecht was still rewriting it (besides those in the other scripts, there are seven separate versions of this song). Eisler's melody for it starts with a quotation from Smetana's *Vltava*.

In the Lorre script Act 2 ends here.

Interlude in the Higher Regions. Stalingrad replaced Rostov on the bound script, and the same with the numerous references that follow up to the end of the play.

Scene 7. Virtually unchanged.

Scene 8. The drunken chaplain was originally not Bullinger's brother but the Reverend Matz from Rosenberg. The relevant amendments were made on the bound script, but the fair copy and the duplicated stage script still have him as Matz. An ironically meant reference to alleged Russian torture chambers was also added, and taken over into the fair copy; after which it was dropped. The price specified in Mrs Kopecka's song 'Come right in and take a seat' (which was accompanied by a melody in Brecht's characteristic notation) was 80 Kreuzers in the bound script; the final cry 'On to Stalingrad!' was missing; and there were a number of other even smaller changes.

Epilogue. Three of the scripts and the duplicated stage script originally had Schweyk saying of the south (p. 137): 'But there are piles of corpses there'.

HITLER
   Then I'll push East.
SCHWEYK
   Then we'll have the British in our hair.

(We have omitted the stage directions.) This is changed to the present reading on the bound script alone; hence it seems likely (as with the references to the London Radio) that Brecht used this script for his final amendments in the 1950s. In the Lorre script (as cited in Knust's *Materialien*) the ending is different from mid-scene on; thus after 'where the front or the rear is' [p. 136] the Führer asks:

Can you tell me, Mr Schweyk, the quickest way to the rear?

SCHWEYK
Excuse me, the way to what?

HITLER
To the rear!

SCHWEYK
Beg to report, sir, this blizzard makes it impossible to hear.

HITLER
Because you're not trying. Just wait; you egotists arouse my fury.

SCHWEYK
Oh, calm down. What's the good of being so gory?

HITLER
I have made history.

SCHWEYK
They'll say 'That's just *his* story'.

HITLER
Don't you realize that ten peoples are now subject to my directing?

SCHWEYK
Not least the Germans, who are supposed to do the subjecting.

HITLER
The average German's useless without my grip to keep him steady.

SCHWEYK
You kicked him too hard when he was down; he's a master race already.

HITLER
When I took over I found his international reputation had been sinking.
Now you and he are fighting side by side.

SCHWEYK
I'd rather he and I were drinking.

HITLER

It was always my assumption that the stronger man had to
win.

SCHWEYK

And so it turned out.

HITLER

Mr Schweyk, if somebody gets done in,

It's because history has decreed he should disappear.

Now take the case of Adam . . .

SCHWEYK

Tell me as we go, or we'll get frozen solid here.

You want a place where you can feel secure.

Right; but the cold may be too much for you to endure.

I can find the way backwards, though, I'm sure I can

Backwards will suit me fine, make me another man.

As for the future, nobody can tell:

What suits me fine may suit you none too well.

But let me lead you now, not that I care:

Without a leader you won't get anywhere.

*Schweyk picks up his rifle and shoves Hitler in front of him. They
stop at the signpost, and Schweyk turns his torch on it. He reads
'Stalingrad—5 km', and marches on in that direction with Hitler
before him. The darkness and the storm swallow them up.*

The final chorus then follows as in our version.